MOTHERS OF SONS

Toward an Understanding of Responsibility

Linda Rennie Forcey

WITHDRAWN

New York
Westport, Connecticut
London

Grateful acknowledgment is made for permission to quote from the following:

Roth, Philip. *Portnoy's Complaint.* New York: Ballantine Books, 1985. Reprinted with permission of Random House, Inc.

Odets, Clifford. "Awake and Sing!" *Masters of Modern Drama.* Edited by Haskell M. Block and Robert G. Shedd. New York: Random House, 1962. Copyright 1933, 1935 by Clifford Odets. Copyright © renewed 1961, 1962 by Clifford Odets. Reprinted with permission of Grove Press, Inc. 196 Houston Street, New York, New York, 10014.

Reprinted from *Expensive People* by Joyce Carol Oates by permission of the publisher, Vanguard Press, Inc. Copyright © 1968 by Joyce Carol Oates.

Parts of Chapter 7 first appeared in the *Christian Science Monitor,* March 15, 1983, p. 23; and in *Women's Studies International Forum,* vol. 7, no. 6, 1984, pp. 447–86.

Library of Congress Cataloging-in-Publication Data

Forcey, Linda Rennie.
    Mothers of sons.

    Bibliography: p.
    Includes index.
    1. Mothers and sons—United States.
2. Motherhood—United States. I. Title.
HQ755.85.F67 1987   306.8'743   86-30331
ISBN 0-275-92323-1 (alk. paper)
ISBN 0-275-92658-3 (pbk. : alk. paper)

Library of Congress Catalog Card Number: 86-30331
ISBN: 0-275-92323-1 (Hb); 0-275-92658-3 (pbk)

First published in 1987

Praeger Publishers, 521 Fifth Avenue, New York, NY 10175
A division of Greenwood Press, Inc.

Printed in the United States of America

The paper used in this book complies with the Permanent Paper Standard issued by the National Information Standards Organization (Z39.48-1984).

10 9 8 7 6 5 4 5 3 2 1

To my husband and children who nurture me

Contents

Acknowledgments

My deepest appreciation and thanks go to the many women who shared their perceptions of their relations with sons. In addition I wish to acknowledge the contribution of the many friends, colleagues, and graduate and undergraduate students who shared their wisdom with me over the years. Special thanks go to Mort Butler, Mary Lou Burrell, and Dianne Wessell who assisted me with the interviewing and transcribing.

With a sabbatical leave and several summer research grants the School of General Studies and Professional Education at the University Center at Binghamton provided the necessary financial support to see the book to conclusion. James Votruba, Harold Nieburg, and Mara Peter-Raoul were among the many colleagues who provided the necessary intellectual encouragement. In addition, the confidence shown by my editor, Alison Podel, made the process of completion a pleasure.

For their enthusiastic interest, support, patience, and individual specialness I shall always be indebted to my children Sally Nash, Peter Adam Nash, Margaret Nash, and Charles Forcey, and to my stepchildren, Blythe and Peter Forcey. Special thanks go to my stepdaughter, Blythe, who read and criticized an earlier version of the book, to Charlie, who with the utmost patience helped me organize on the computer the data from the interviews, and to Peter Adam Nash who dialogued with me from start to finish, offering invaluable suggestions along the way. To my husband, Pete, I find no adequate way to say thanks — for his unflagging love, encouragement, and support, his nurturing of our children and me, his listening, his reading and rereading of draft after draft, his invaluable criticism and superb editorial skills. I just hope he knows.

1

INTRODUCTION

None of us can hope to solve our basic problems: why we are alive, how we should be born, behave, think, love, labor, die. But, on the other hand, women now more than ever cannot afford to disregard the task of understanding themselves. . . . A drive to self-knowledge is more than the dilatory self-interested pastime of the so-called liberated woman. It is a serious human enterprise. It is a protest against the dehumanization of society made by women on behalf of everyone, because it is women who find themselves most discomforted by the gap between who they are and what they are supposed to be.

Ann Oakley (1)

THE PROBLEM

Mothers of sons have been placed in a catch-22 situation. In the eyes of our social commentators they have been damned if they do and damned if they don't. While Freud, his followers, practically every biographer of famous men, most social scientists, and literary figures too, tell us that behind every conqueror, every hero, is *the* responsible mother, they usually describe her as overinvolved, overwhelming, and smothering. In contrast we are told that behind every vain, hypersensitive, invidious, cruel, violent, schizophrenic, paranoid, sexually deviant, narcissistic, over-achieving, or merely unfulfilled male of whatever age there is that same responsible mother.

Curiously, in these times of change and aggravated tension between the sexes, the mother-son relationship from mothers' perspectives has

1

been virtually unexamined by social scientists and by mothers themselves, including, until very recently, feminists. Social scientists for a long time have had a great deal to say about the effect of the mother upon the son, the mother constituting the key variable in the determination of the personality and character of the son. But they have had little to say about the effect of the son upon the mother. Their literature has offered little to help us understand her because it has focused on an ill-defined, unquestioned reification for all times and places of the female who bears a son. (2)

Feminist scholarship from the late 1960s through the 1970s dealt primarily with the materialistic oppression of women, encouraging them to relinquish their traditional role of nurturers to pursue political and economic equality. It played down, until recently, the significance of sex and gender distinction, the unconscious, the irrational, the unique, and the paradoxical in human relationships, with one notable exception, mother-daughter relationships. There feminists felt comfortable. When feminists dealt with mother-son relationships, it was usually as an aside in the context of other issues such as the family and the institution of motherhood in general. Such asides usually sought to explain how and why mothers have not lived up to their responsibility.

Through the 1960s and early 1970s, few voices from mothers of sons themselves were heard. It was as though something were blocking social scientists, feminists, and all mothers from approaching the subject with the open-mindedness they had recently begun to apply to other relationships; a taboo topic, it seemed. But common sense dictates that the mother-son relationships from mothers' perspectives can no longer be ignored. In fact, with the majority of mothers now in the workplace, much of the current tension, fear, and uncertainty about the future of the family and societal values focuses on the role of the mother, reflecting the anxiety felt by both women and men over who is going to be responsible, who is going to mother the men of tomorrow, who or what is going to provide that haven for men in a heartless world.

This book is about the mother-son relationship from the perspectives of mothers alone. One of its major assumptions is that only when we can begin to listen to mothers of sons as individuals with histories, human needs, strengths, and weaknesses grappling with an impossible responsibility can we come to terms with the war between the sexes. This is not to say there are not other sides. Of course there are. They, however, are not the focus of this study.

Readers will undoubtedly find themselves at times, as I did, on *terra incognita*. The subject matter is what mothers have to say about their relationships with their sons, their raw personal experiences; that is, what they consciously know, feel, and choose to share with us. It is hoped that you will assume with William James that life *is* experience. The experiential approach assumes that if we know mothers' of sons orientation to their outer world we shall have taken the necessary first step toward an understanding of the essential nature of their relationship with their sons.

You are challenged to put yourselves into the lives of these women, to try to see the world as these women see it. Naturally, you are also challenged to reconstruct themes, to read between the lines, to tie together the threads, to explain. And simultaneously, while searching for the commonalities and patterns of these women's stories you are challenged to assess the intrusion of your own life experiences as daughters or sons, mothers or fathers, as well as those of mine as author. We all, of course, will be uniquely interpreting along the way.

The book is grounded in the oral histories of over 100 women from a wide variety of socioeconomic backgrounds. By encouraging women in all their diversity to speak for themselves about the critical mother-son relationship it is my hope that social consciousness as to what it means for mothers to raise sons in this age of tension over mothering and gender roles will be heightened. It is also my hope that men will come to have a better understanding of the variety of mothering patterns out of which they have emerged. The primary objective of this book is to do for mothers of sons what Nancy Seifer's *Nobody Speaks for Me* and Lillian Ruben's *Worlds of Pain* did for working-class women. (3) That is, by making conscious the complexity of women's own experiences as mothers of sons, the book will help all of us to identify ourselves in our uniqueness as well as in our commonality. The problem is that mothers of sons have not yet been heard, and they need to be.

The central question around which the book focuses is how do mothers perceive their relationships with their sons? That is, what do they have to tell us about the relationship, and their responsibility to and for it? In order to refine our understanding of mothers' perceptions of the relationship, several subsidiary questions must also be embedded in our search for understanding. Why has the mother-son relationship from mothers' perspectives been ignored? Do women consider themselves to be fundamentally different from men; and, if so, in what ways? What do women have to say about the mothering responsibility in general, irrespective of the sex of their children? Do mothers perceive their responsibility for the mothering of sons as different from their responsibility for the mothering of daughters? How do women's attitudes toward men affect their attitudes toward their sons? In what ways do the influences of class, age, marital status and satisfaction, employment status and satisfaction, personality, and other variables affect these perceptions? What impact has the women's movement had on views on mothering in general and mothering of sons in particular? And finally, do any commonalities or patterns to mothers' perceptions emerge from this study?

Some definitions are in order. In this book, *mothers* are those women who perceive themselves to have assumed willingly the responsibility for the nurturing and socialization of their biological, adopted, or stepchildren. The focus is on mothers' *perception* of the relationship. How mothers perceive themselves and their responsibility in their relationship with their sons is defined in terms of what they say about that responsibility. This definition of perception reflects another underlying assumption of the book: a person's own story is and must be the initial guide to an understanding of the patterns of her existence. The use of the term *responsibility* with respect to the mothering of sons means that the mother is held, in a primary way, answerable and accountable for the well-being of her sons. Although this book focuses on the obligations implicit in kinship, the *relationship* between mothers and sons is viewed more broadly as a process of connection and involvement; one that, as with all intimate interpersonal contacts, involves love, conflict, giving, receiving, growing, and changing over time with the realities of living.

Because this book is written from a feminist perspective (the very word feminism has since the late nineteenth century when it was coined so polarized those who feel attachment to it and those antagonistic to it), a definition of *feminism* is useful. A general working one with which I am comfortable assumes the historical oppression of women and stresses the interrelationship of theory and practice to eliminate it:

> Feminism is both a way of thinking about the world, and a way of acting in it. . . . [It] is a perspective that views gender as one of the most important bases of the structure and organization of the social world. Feminists argue that in most known societies this structure has granted women lower status and value, more limited access to valuable resources, and less autonomy and opportunity to make choices over their lives than it has granted men. Feminists further believe that although this gender-based world may be

organized around certain biological facts such as the exclusive capacity of men to create sperm and the exclusive capacity of women to bear children, gender inequality is due to the social construction of human experience, which means that it should be possible to eradicate it.

Associated with this definition is a prescription; feminism is a movement for social change through solidarity:

[F]eminists believe that these inequities should be eliminated and that to do this, feminists cannot simply try to do better as individuals in the social world as it exists, but must work together to change the structure of the social world. Any other action means making the best of an unjust situation. (4)

THE GENESIS

Because of the experiential nature of this book you may wish to have an understanding of the experiences from which the focus emerges. The focus did not emerge, as one might expect, from my own experiences with sons. Like most mothers of sons I was quite silent on that relationship. Although I have long been in the process of raising (with the help of my husband) three of them (one of whom is a stepson) as well as three daughters (one of whom is a stepdaughter), it was not until I was deeply involved in this book that I realized the significance of taking a close introspective look at myself and those relationships.

Instead, I first began to reflect about the mother-son relationship in 1971 when I returned to graduate school after child-bearing and -raising for more than a decade. My Ph.D. dissertation, entitled "Personality in Politics: The Commitment of a Suicide," was a search for meaning in the life of one young man who killed himself at the age of 31. (5) He had been a "red diaper baby," a prominent political activist of the 1960s, a scholar, and a personal friend of mine. Through analysis of the young man's letters, personal papers, diaries, and open-ended interviews with his friends, fellow activists, colleagues, lovers, and family, particularly his mother, I attempted to tell from many different perspectives the story of the complicated interplay between one man's personal life and his political-socioeconomic environment.

As I worked on the project, interviewing family and friends, I experienced a shifting relationship of myself to my subject. At the start I had cared deeply about my lost friend, and I was fascinated by his father, a prominent ex-Communist and scholar. Before I had even met the mother I had wondered about her and her relationship with her son as others had. So did the mother herself, I later learned, for the suicide of a son symbolizes the ultimate failure of mothering.

Over the years as I pondered this man's life something, indeed, was happening. I found myself often becoming angry with my subject, my former friend, and angrier still with his father. And I found myself becoming increasingly concerned with his mother, so much so that in my mind she, as much as her son, was a victim. Being one of those social scientists who believes that all inquiry is, to some extent, autobiographical, I was aware that this shifting relationship of myself to those I was studying was not occurring in a vacuum. My developing feminist consciousness and my own children's emergence into adolescence was enhancing my empathy for all mothers. I found myself wanting to understand better that particular mother whose son, my friend, had killed himself. I found myself wanting to better understand the relationships of all mothers to sons. Erik Erikson's admonition to social scientists came to mind: "Our ability to see others clearly depends . . . upon our readiness to take a hard introspective view of ourselves." (6) But I knew that when it came to this relationship I, as a social scientist and mother of sons, was blocked. And so were many others, I suspected. Out of my desire to contribute to feminist theory an understanding of the complexity of this particular mother's tragic experience, and the experiences of many mothers, I turned to this present exploration.

CONCEPTUAL FRAMEWORK AND METHODOLOGY

This study is grounded in a commitment to an interdisciplinary approach for the social sciences, to feminism, and to social justice in all its forms. There is no one set of generalizations to which the research problem presented here has reference. As I see it, the goal is ultimately humanistic; an attempt to understand the common core of existential yearnings that is the fate of humankind.

We need to learn to be unafraid to listen to the other side, the side that has yet to be heard, the voices of mothers of sons. Thus the underlying conceptual framework is on a "phenomenological" plane. Phenomenology is the method of existentialism. For an existentialist, as Gordon Allport tells us,

To understand another human being one must grasp the other's subjective view of life because the phenomena of his [her] experience are the very heart of his [her] existence. How he [she] perceives his [her] surroundings, how he [she] fashions his [her] assumptive world, what anxieties, meanings, aspirations compose his [her] world view — all these are the phenomenological data upon which existential analysis rests. (7)

As noted, this book is about how women perceive their relationships with their sons, that is, what they consciously and subjectively choose to convey to me, the researcher, about the nature of that relationship, their responsibility to it and for it. The issues of daily life, connections and involvement, love and conflict, growing, changing, giving and receiving from their perspectives are what are involved. The book is not about how husbands perceive their wives' relationship with their sons, or how sons perceive their mothers' relationships to them. (A husband of one of the women interviewed confronted me on the street one day, demanding I give him a chance to tell his side of the story. I told him it wasn't his turn. My own sons swear they are going to write a best-seller called *Sons and Feminist Mothers*.)

Because the purpose of the study is to enhance our understanding of mothers' perceptions, the primary methodology used is and must be that of empathetic listening. Such listening means trying to see the other's point of view in a caring way and letting her know that what she believes really matters.

Empathetic listening is oral history, as I have come to define it. (8) Oral history, particularly as used by feminists, is a method that encourages a humanistic approach to the social sciences by forcing us to recognize the creativity of everywoman and everyman and by challenging all stereotypes. The sharing of what William James calls those "personal secrets" is the sharing of the phenomena of our very existence, our experiences that highlight both the uniqueness and the commonality of all of us.

In his penetrating analysis of *Oral History and Delinquency: The Rhetoric of Criminology*, James Bennett argues that oral history, by its very nature, occupies an area somewhere between theory and action, a "marginal" space between the individual and his or her environment, the middle ground between the universal and the particular. (9) Oral history is marginal in another sense too. It serves as a bridge between groups that need to communicate because they do not quite seem to fit into the scheme of things. Marginality in this multidimensional sense is the key characteristic of the oral history approach of this book.

Oral history as a marginal method may be viewed, according to Bennett, as "pre-predictive," the stage of research that precedes and underlies the formation of propositions and hypotheses. Of course assumptions are never absent; they are, however, left freely inexplicit. The aim of oral history is to perceive patterns in people's perceptions of reality while being ever cautious that underlying assumptions do not produce another set of hardened stereotypes.

It is actually the value of "rhetoric," the natural eloquence of first-hand accounts of experiences, that makes oral history a method essential to our understanding of the perceptions of mothers of sons. This appeals to our common sense and suggests new questions, new processes, new areas of research. Doing oral history requires, as Ann Oakley has argued, that "the mythology of 'hygienic' research with its accompanying mystification of the researcher and the researched as objective instruments of data production be replaced by the recognition that personal involvement is more than dangerous bias — it is the condition under which people come to know each other and to admit others into their lives." (10)

Therefore, the conceptual framework of this book on how mothers perceive their relationships with their sons is based on an interdisciplinary, feminist perspective that utilizes the method of oral history to open up a new world of phenomena in the lives of women. It takes a phenomenological approach because I believe that what these women tell us about their experiences as mothers of sons has its own validity.

RESEARCH DESIGN

The research design centers on the open-ended interview. The purpose of the interviews, which are really conversations, is to find out things about mothers of sons that cannot be otherwise discovered; things like feelings, thoughts, and intentions.

The interviewing process began in May 1980. An advertisement calling for volunteers who wished to talk about their relationships with their sons was placed in a monthly news and activities letter written and circulated across New York state's southern tier by a continuing education program for women at a large state university The initial responses were from women who indicated some interest in furthering their education; the snowballing effect was unexpected, eventually bringing forth calls from several hundred women of all ages from a variety of class, racial, ethnic, and demographic backgrounds.

From the list of respondents I selected 12 women from varying ethnic-economic backgrounds for exploratory conversations. These pilot interviews were unstructured. I approached these women with little advance effort to formulate presuppositions as to what might be learned, rather permitting the conversations to flow freely. The interviews, usually taped in the women's homes, lasted between one and three hours. The women were given the opportunity to schedule another appointment with me if they desired and approximately one-third did.

From analysis of the emerging themes of these conversations an interview guide was prepared. The purpose of the guide was to secure some degree of uniformity in the information being collected. The guide was intentionally unspecific, merely listing subject areas upon which the conversation would touch if appropriate. At the same time great leeway was left for individual experiences and perspectives to emerge.

Two graduate students, both mothers of sons enrolled in an interdisciplinary master's program after many years of being homemakers, assisted me with the interviews. In order to ensure a common style among us, the students first listened to one of my pilot interviews. Then I interviewed them and they in turn interviewed me. (The information they elicited from me during these interviews proved to be extremely useful as I reflected on my own relationship with sons.) We then compared, contrasted, and analyzed the results. We agreed to guide the flow of conversation only gently, to keep the emphasis always on listening rather than on asking preformulated questions. Similarly they and I responded in a sharing way to questions asked of us.

The general areas covered included: biographical data on the mothers (age, family, class, religion, race, ethnicity, education, employment history, marital status, number, age, and sex of children); mothers' perceptions of their relationships with their own siblings and parents; their relationships with the father of their sons; their sons' relationship with their fathers, and their own relationships with their sons; their relationship with their daughters as compared with their sons (where applicable); their expectations for their sons and for the relationship. Also included were mothers' opinions on the mothering role as traditionally defined, on the women's movement, and on changing roles of women.

Following the pilot studies, 102 more interviews were conducted by myself and the two assistants. Because of limited resources the sampling method became purposeful. As we worked with the original respondents to the advertisement as well as others who had heard about the study through friends, we attempted to get in touch with women of all kinds, particularly so as to avoid class and race bias. Nine percent of the women interviewed were of minorities in an area where blacks, orientals, and other minorities are a disproportionately small part of the population.

As to the variables incorporated in the guide, we felt that the age of mothers was significant because it would usually (but not always) reflect the ages of sons, the amount of time mothers had been experiencing the relationships, and the stages of life and historical periods which they and their sons had traversed. The women were divided, as of the time of the first interview, into five age categories: 18–25; 26–35; 36–45; 46–55; and 56–75. As the selection method became increasingly purposeful we concentrated, to maximize depth of experience, on women with sons over 16. The stories we ultimately decided to share with you in more detail are those from women in the third and fourth categories (ages 36–55). These we (over 36 ourselves) concluded were the mothers with the most to tell us.

The second and third main variables were whether or not the mother was, or had been, or intended to be, employed outside the home, and whether she was married, or had been, or was intending to be, to the father of her son or sons. The pilot conversations had already suggested that these circumstances might be major factors underlying variations in accounts of the relationship given.

Categories by class appeared to be another essential variable to our understanding of the mothers. The initial conversations led us to expect significant differences related to class in the experiences of mothering of sons. For the interview guide the rough classification of working, middle, and upper class seemed sufficient for the gradations of status that phenomenologically, if not theoretically, are widely and readily perceived. (The degree to which in recent times explicit class identification occurs in the media is notable.) Nevertheless, since the subjects of our research were women, three massive changes in American social life of the past few decades made us extremely cautious about accepting rigid definitions of social class made in the literature of social science. (11) The first of these was the vast openings of educational opportunities at all levels to women of all ages and their widespread utilization. The second change was the further movement of women into employment outside the home since the 1950s, up 170 percent. And the third change was the ever-increasing number of single female-headed households. These changes have made the element of class status of all women extraordinarily fluid, certainly not one that could be determined merely by the nature of the husband's job or his income level.

Obviously, in trying to formulate more precise classifications for levels of social status the need was again to listen, to determine how women themselves perceived their place in a society that, for them particularly, had been undergoing dramatic change. Thus our first rule of thumb for the study was to place women in whatever categories they perceived themselves to be. If during an interview a mother indicated in any way that she considered herself to be part of the lower (usually perceived as "working"), middle or upper class, we accepted that self-categorization without reservations. Phenomenologically considered, such a subjective perception of status was likely to be, in fact, the active variable in the mother-son relationship whatever the objective realities.

Frequently, however, the subject of class identification did not come up because the interviewer felt it would be intrusive or offensive to ask — direct questions of this nature being out of keeping with the tone of the interview. For such cases, we defined class categories for the purpose of this study in the following manner. If a woman was on welfare (and gave no indication as to self-perceived status) we classified her as within an "under" division of the working class. If she had no more than a high school education and she and/or her husband worked in traditionally defined blue-collar jobs we considered her to be working class.

There were, interestingly, a significant number of women with recent college and even graduate degrees who perceived themselves as working class. Several laughingly told us that their working-class parents would be horrified to hear their educated children so define themselves and would probably attribute it to the bad influence of leftist professors who glorified the working class. For these women, by our rule concerning self-perception, we accepted their own categorization.

Middle-class status, for those who gave no indication, was accorded to employed women in white-collar or lower- to middle-rank professional positions. For those not employed, the husband's (or father's of sons) occupation was used as the best rough guide. Predictably, the majority of those participating in the study considered themselves middle class.

An approximate measure of upper-class status emerged from the interviews. Upper-class women were those who clearly indicated they had no financial worries and (financial aid thus not a consideration) sent their sons to private schools. Also included were those in top-ranking, high-income business or professional positions, or those whose husbands held such positions.

As with the pilots, these interviews were taped in the women's homes and usually took between one and three hours, with the opportunity to meet again if they wished to share further perceptions. One-fourth of the women interviewed did. The participants were assured that their interviews would be confidential with names and other identifying factors changed.

Although the interview guide served to provide some focus for the conversations, we, as interviewers, made certain that the conversation flowed naturally within the women's own frameworks. We were also sensitive to the fact that our presence was shaping the content as well as the form of the interview. We, therefore, asked few direct questions, took care to be nonjudgmental, and felt free to share our own experiences when asked by the women to do so or when we deemed it appropriate.

With detail-oriented, elaboration, and clarification probes (such as "How did you feel?" or "When did that happen?" or "Why were you frustrated?") we were usually able to maintain sufficient control of the interview so that it covered the rough areas of the guide. But not always. The question of how far to probe sensitive areas (including even age) plagues all interviewers; we allowed common sense and perception of the specific individual to guide us. As a consequence, not all of our areas of inquiry were covered for all women.

After the completion of an interview, we made summaries of the contents of the tapes according to our broad categories. We also noted our own overall impressions of the interview (for example: "open and relaxed, conversation flowed freely and comfortably," or "mother appeared uncomfortable discussing marital relationship," or "mother seemed to want to discuss only daughter"), our own sense of the mother's relationship with the son, and the major theme or themes upon which the mother chose to focus. This information was then coded to help organize and analyze data. Three graduate students not involved in the interviewing process, one male and two female, assisted with the coding. The tapes were then either fully transcribed or partially transcribed with summaries of repetitious or irrelevant material. The transcripts were edited where necessary for clarity.

Working out the best way to analyze and interpret the women's stories was a difficult and ongoing process. There are no clear-cut rules about how to proceed, how to make sense of it all. Yet analysis and interpretation mark the challenge and the opportunity for creativity in oral history. From the initial interviews to the final one, and from the first outline to the final written word of the manuscript, new topics and patterns, and connections among them, were being collected, labeled, and filed. There was a constant working back and forth between the interview data and the emerging categories, with repeated returns to interviews to insure an accurate account of women's perceptions.

Such "experiential analysis" brings its surprises. For example, we discovered that many mothers of post-adolescent sons wanted their sons to join the military, often actively encouraged them to do so. Mothers' views on military training for their sons was not one of our early envisaged categories. It was not until we had begun the arduous process of finding and ordering patterns that the centrality of the military for many overwhelmed mothers of sons became clear. From this product of listening there developed in turn one important issue at the very heart of the study, that of the awesomeness of maternal responsibility. We had not thought initially to ask how many women found "joining up" to be the solution to their sons' problems. But here they were in the transcripts, first merely particular individuals, and then in aggregate, bearers of a recurrent theme suggesting new questions.

Another product of experiential analysis was the aforementioned concentration on older mothers with sons aged at least 16. (These are sometimes called the "invisible women"; that is, those no longer young enough to be noticed in a crowd.) I came to realize that although I had learned a great deal from women with young sons the richness and depth of living in a relationship over a number of years were missing. Perhaps too, my own age and that of my sons provided an extra measure of illuminating empathy with these "invisible women."

It is the very complexity of the process required to analyze and interpret oral history that makes the method indispensable for new fields of inquiry, such as the lives of everyday mothers of sons. As already noted, oral history cannot conclusively "prove" a theory. It constitutes the "pre-predictive" stage of research. It is a rhetorically effective way of raising new questions about issues that often concern people who would otherwise be ignored. Therefore, the goal of analysis and interpretation must be to achieve a delicate balance between what is unique and what is common to the lives of those being studied.

It is in this pre-predictive sense, one with no claim to being *the* fact or *the* truth, that this book essays an investigative contribution to feminist theory. Its focus on the rhetoric of mothers of sons reflects an effort to dereify them, to make them human. The emerging themes and patterns they themselves brought forth and they now form the organization of the study. These themes and patterns find the reality of mothering sons in the ways women themselves see it.

The book is divided into eight chapters. A selective review of the literature on mothers of sons with an emphasis on feminist studies is presented in Chapter 2, "Silent Jocastas." Although the literature of the social sciences offers little from mothers' perspectives on women's relationships with sons, it does suggest the cultural imperatives of our times within which women have had to carry on mothering. It forms, therefore, the glowering backdrop of mothers' perceptions of the relationship. Such cultural imperatives also color feminist analyses of mothering experiences as is shown in the discussion of selected widely-read feminist works that touch upon the mother-son theme.

The message of Chapter 3, "The Awesome Responsibility," and broadly speaking the entire book, is that both the conventional themes and revised feminist interpretations of the responsibility of mothers for the well-being of sons is personally and politically damaging for both women and men. The excerpts from interviews reflect the wide range of ways in which women define their responsibility and grapple with it over time. Chapter 4, "Expectations," shows that, contrary to the testimonies of Sigmund Freud, Simone de Beauvoir, and Alex Portnoy, mothers do not invariably have the great expectations for sons they are assumed to have. The variables of class, age, personalities, and relationships with daughters are highlighted.

Chapter 5, "Communicating," focuses on the ways in which mothers perceive the communication process with their sons. It is argued that women generally do communicate "in a different voice," one markedly more caring in tone and content than that of men. However, because of the nature of their perceived responsibility toward sons they often speak in yet another voice to them. It is a conciliatory voice, marked by such affectivities as peace at any price, fear of confrontation, suppressed anger, and rigid limitations on the sharing of experiences.

Mothers of sons give us good ground for questioning much that we have heard from the novelist, the psychoanalyst, and the social scientist regarding women's attitudes toward their sons' girlfriends/partners/wives. In Chapter 6, "Sons and Lovers," they tell us they do not view their sons as substitute lovers, they do want their sons to love women other than themselves, and they have affection and empathy for their sons' lovers.

Chapter 7, "Turning to Uncle Sam," is about the many tired, frustrated, or otherwise overwhelmed mothers of sons who encourage their sons to join the military because they believe there is no place else to turn. The focus once again is on the awesome, for many almost impossible, responsibility of mothers for the welfare of their sons. There are two additional themes: our military recruiters are very much aware of these supporters; and feminists are not because we have not been listening to these mothers. From four portraits and several brief excerpts from interviews the reader will come to understand that women who encourage their sons to enlist must be listened to, not castigated. These women want their sons to have self-discipline, maturity, training and skills, an education, a job. It is their perception that there is no place else for them to turn but the military.

The concluding chapter, "Jocastas Unbound," pulls together the themes of the earlier ones to show that there is, indeed, another point of view on the mother-son relationship — that of mothers themselves with changing perceptions of their responsibilities. The chapter includes excerpts of stories from women who have broken the silence, have shattered the mother-son myth. Mothers talk about their relationships with their sons as human beings to human beings with all their variables interacting over time. Key factors are the impact of the women's movement in the United States and the increasing participation of women in institutions of higher learning and in the labor market. An analysis of the themes and connections emerging from this study show that only when we begin to listen to mothers of sons will we then be ready to consider the central question for the late 1980s, the one that frightens us all: Who is going to nurture the men of tomorrow?

NOTES

1. Ann Oakley, *Taking It Like a Woman* (London: Fontana Paperbacks, 1985), p. 2.

2. Although Robert Nisbet (*Prejudices: A Philosophical Dictionary* [Cambridge, Mass.: Harvard University Press, 1982], p. 258), probably did not have motherhood in mind, his definition of reification is useful:

The Oxford English Dictionary lists the word *reif* (or *rieff*) just before *reification*, defining it as the act of robbery or as the one who commits robbery. Reification is in its own way robbery: the stealing of life from the individual and the concrete in order to secrete it in some ontological invertebrate. Considering the combination of robbery and violence, the act of reifying may be likened to mugging.

3. Nancy Seifer, *Nobody Speaks for Me: Self-Portraits of American Working Class Women* (New York: Simon and Schuster, 1976); and Lillian Breslow Ruben, *Worlds of Pain: Life in the Working Class Family* (New York: Basic Books, 1976).
4. Virginia Sapiro, *Women in American Society* (Palo Alto, Ca.: Mayfield, 1986), pp. 440–41.
5. Linda Rennie Forcey, "Personality in Politics: The Commitment of a Suicide" (Ph.D. diss., State University of New York at Binghamton, 1978).
6. Erik Erikson, "The First Psychoanalyst," *Yale Review* (Autumn 1965), p. 60.
7. Gordon Allport, *Letters From Jenny* (New York: Harcourt Brace Jovanovich, 1965), p. 175.
8. See James Bennett, *Oral History and Delinquency: The Rhetoric of Criminology* (Chicago: University of Chicago Press, 1981); Sherna Gluck, "What's So Special About Women? Women's Oral History," *Frontiers* 2, no. 2 (1977), pp. 1–17; Susan H. Armitage, "The Next Step," *Frontiers* 7, no. 1 (1983), pp. 3–8; Ann Oakley, "Interviewing Women: A Contradiction in Terms," in *Doing Feminist Research,* ed. Helen Roberts (London: Routledge & K. Paul, 1981), pp. 30–61.
9. As a sociological term, "marginality" was first defined by Robert E. Park in 1928: "The individual who through migration, education, marriage, or some other influence leaves one social group or culture without making a satisfactory adjustment to another finds himself on the margin of each but a member of neither. He is a 'marginal man.'" In Everett V. Stonequist, *Marginal Man* (New York: Charles Scribner's Sons, 1937), pp. 2–3.
10. Oakley, "Interviewing Women," p. 58.
11. For discussions on the complexities of defining class see, for example: C. Wright Mills, *White Collar* (New York: Oxford University Press, 1951); Harold L. Wilensky, "Mass Society and Mass Culture: Interdependence or Independence," *American Sociological Review* 29 (1964), pp. 173–97; Stanley Aronowitz, *False Promises* (New York: McGraw-Hill, 1973); Harry Braverman, *Labor and Monopoly Capitalism: The Degradation of Work in the Twentieth Century* (New York: Monthly Review Press, 1974); Rubin, *Worlds of Pain*; and Ann Ferguson, "On Conceiving Motherhood and Sexuality: A Feminist Materialist Approach," in *Mothering: Essays in Feminist Theory,* ed. Joyce Trebilcot (Totowa, N.J.: Rowman & Allanheld, 1983).

2
SILENT JOCASTAS

> These are not *natural* silences — what Keats called *agonie ennuyeuse* (the tedious agony) — that necessary time for renewal, lying fallow, gestation, in the natural cycle of creation. The silences I speak of here are unnatural: the unnatural thwarting of what struggles to come into being, but cannot.
>
> *Tillie Olsen* (1)

JOCASTA AND OEDIPUS

Social scientists have had a great deal to say about the effect of the mother upon the son. (2) The themes, growing primarily out of Freudian psychoanalytic theory, revolve around the assumption of a unique tension in the relationship provoked by an all-powerful, loving, but seductively castrating mother who causes considerable anxiety and pain to her son.

Social scientists have developed a symbolic vocabulary that pigeonholes and stereotypes mothers of sons, thereby denying them the complexity of thought, feeling, and deed that is granted others. (3) Despite qualifications that sometimes appear in the literature on the relationship, we have all come to know who is responsible, who is the guilty one. (4) We (men and women) have absorbed, with the help of psychoanalysis, the Oedipus myth. Women until recently have been silenced by their absorption of it while men have been granted a sublime alibi.

On the face of it this seems absurd. Why, when there are thousands of myths, should this particular Greek legend of Oedipus Rex who slew his father and married his mother have seized our human imaginations? Why has Oedipus become a household word? Why should mothers be silenced and scapegoated by the fate of this particular mother? It could be said that the struggle for a more fully developed response to these questions is what contemporary feminist scholarship is all about. But more on this subject later.

The Greeks believed in fate. One's future was predestined for the most part, a concept scarcely conducive to self-improvement. We with a Judeo-Christian heritage are struck by the concept that the *act,* rather than the intent or circumstance, appears to be everything. Oedipus was doomed before he was born. No matter what he did circumstances brought him closer and closer to his preordained fate. Oedipus was an innocent victim of the gods as, according to psychoanalytic theory, are our sons who dream of their mothers, impelled by the oracle or inner voice to the incestuous impulses of childhood.

Although the Greeks believed in fate, there were also ethical considerations. In the story of Oedipus and Jocasta there had been a crime for which retribution was to be extracted. It turns out that Laius, father of Oedipus and husband of Jocasta, had abducted a young male named Chrysippus, and was doomed by the gods to be killed for his homosexuality if he were to have a son. (5) Because of this curse Laius refuses to sleep with Jocasta. She, wanting a child, resorts to "raping" her husband when he is drunk. Then, when the child from this union is three days old the king, in an abortive attempt to avert his destiny, orders his wife to bind the son's feet and leave him to die from exposure on a mountain top.

From this point on in the legend Jocasta's role in the circumstances of her son's life appears to be innocent. Oedipus, as you probably recall, is found by a shepherd and taken to the king of Corinth who raises him as his own son. Then, when Oedipus reaches manhood the god Apollo tells him that he is fated to kill his father and marry his mother. Believing the king of Corinth to be his true father, he wanders to Thebes in an attempt to avert his fate. At the gates of the city he kills in self-defense a cruel driver and his master as well, who turns out to be the young man's true father, King Laius. Then, entering Thebes, he solves the riddle of the sphinx, thereby liberating the city from terrible suffering. The grateful citizens of Thebes offer him their kingdom as well as the dead King Laius's widow who is, of course, none other than Oedipus's natural mother, Jocasta. Not for many years (and several children) later do the gods reveal to Oedipus the terrible truth of his relationship with Jocasta.

Oedipus must blind himself and be banished from the kingdom and Jocasta, whose role had been passive throughout, must kill herself.

ENTER FREUD

Sigmund Freud, whose mind became extremely excited by the drama of the Greeks, connected the conflicts of the tragedians with those in his own life and in the lives of his patients. Particularly beguiling to him was this story of Oedipus Rex. He created an enduring mythical language from it. Oedipus (and, indirectly, Jocasta) came alive and he convinced us that "It isn't only that we possess the same desires and fears [as the Greeks] . . . but that we, like they, spend a lifetime coming to terms with those desires and fears and do so in relatively similar ways." (6)

Freud saw the Oedipus myth as legend growing out of the unconscious desire of all sons to possess their mothers and murder their fathers. Of Oedipus Freud wrote: "His fate moves us only because it might have been our own, because the oracle laid upon us before our birth the very curse which rested upon him." Like Oedipus, Freud continued,

> [it] may be that we were all destined to direct our first sexual impulses toward our mothers, and our first impulses of hatred and resistance toward our fathers; our dreams convince us that we were. . . . Like Oedipus, we live in ignorance of the desires that offend morality, the desires that nature has forced upon us. (7)

The legend, as we know, became the centerpiece of Freud's theory of the development of personality, the heart of psychoanalysis. According to the theory, until the age of four or five little boys love their mothers and identify with their fathers. Then during the phallic period when their sexual urge increases, they incestuously crave their mothers and view their fathers as rivals. If all goes well, by about the age of 12 they resolve their Oedipal wishes by repressing their incestuous desires for their mother, thus becoming stable heterosexual men. If all does not go well in so resolving their Oedipal yearnings, they become neurotic.

Freud's focus was on Oedipus and the father-son conflict; not Jocasta and the mother-son conflict. That Freud chose that focus reflects what many consider to be his major blind spot. (8) Freud maintained an extremely close relationship with his mother, into her nineties and his seventies, and he had ambivalent, often hostile feelings toward his father. Perhaps he was not able to come to terms with these feelings within himself. Sociologist Philip Slater argues that Freud's comment that the mother-son relationship was "least liable to disaster," one giving the "purest examples of unchanging tenderness, undisturbed by any egoistic consideration," was "surely the most inaccurate statement he ever made — a breathtaking piece of sentimental denial by a man rarely given to it." (9)

The implications of this "blind spot" for our understanding of mothers of sons are significant. Consider this statement from the father of psychoanalysis comparing his male and female patients:

> A man of about thirty strikes us as a youthful, somewhat unformed individual, whom we expect to make powerful use of the possibilities for development opened up to him by analysis. A woman of the same age, however, often frightens us by her psychical rigidity, and unchangeability. Her libido has taken up final positions and seems incapable of exchanging them for others. There are no paths open to further development; it is as though the whole process had already run its course and remains thenceforward insusceptible to influence — as though, indeed, the difficult development to femininity had exhausted the possibilities of the person concerned. (10)

Within Freud's context, we might ask ourselves how we can possibly begin to understand mothers of sons when they at 30 are defined as *woman,* psychically rigid and unchangeable with no paths open to further development?

The literature on Oedipus Rex, after Freud, continues to center on the father-son conflict although it is but a small part of the myth — the story is primarily that of a mother-son marriage. This to be sure has more to do with the history of female oppression and the nature of psychoanalytic thought than the actual content of the myth. However, we need not belabor this patriarchal bias. (11) Rather the point is to draw attention to the implications of the starkly compelling Oedipal language, with its many ambiguities, for mothers of sons. "If the Oedipus Rex is capable of moving a modern reader or playgoer no less powerfully than it moved the contemporary Greeks," Freud reasoned, "the only possible explanation is that the effect of the Greek tragedy does not depend upon the conflict between fate and human will, but upon the peculiar nature of the material by which this conflict is revealed. *There must be a voice within us which is prepared to acknowledge the compelling power of fate in the Oedipus.*" (12)

A slippery, murky sensation envelops us when we contemplate the relationship Jocasta had with her son. Did Jocasta, like Oedipus, really live in ignorance of the desires that nature had forced upon her? Or did she know what was happening? What *did* Sophocles mean when he had Jocasta comforting her son/husband Oedipus with the following lines?

> As to your mother's marriage bed,
> Don't fear it,
> Before this, in dreams too, as well as oracles,
> Many a man has lain with his mother.
> But he to whom such things are nothing bears his life
> most easily. (13)

There is tyranny for mothers of sons in the symbolism of this myth. Norman O. Brown, the provocative neo-Freudian classicist, tells us that an appreciation of symbolism is the key to an understanding of the phenomenal world:

> To make in ourselves a new consciousness, an erotic sense of reality, is to become conscious of symbolism. Symbolism is mind making connections (correspondences) rather than distinctions (separations). Symbolism makes conscious interconnections and unions that were unconscious and repressed. Freud says, symbolism is on the track of a former identity, a lost unity. (14)

But here are two of the symbols Brown offers mothers of sons:

> The vagina is a devouring mouth, or vagina dentata; the jaws of the giant cannibalistic mother, a menstruating woman with the penis bitten off, a bleeding trophy. (15)

> The stone phallus, a permanent erection. The Milky Way is really a mother and her son stuck together forever in the act of copulation; a pair of dogs connected by the male dog's penis and tail, which are permanently fixed in the bitch's anus. But to be stuck (in a rut) is also castration. (16)

SOCIAL SCIENTISTS ON MOTHERS OF SONS

The literature of the social sciences explores the mother-son relationship primarily within a post-Freudian context that argues for the centrality of the mother-child relationship in the development of the personality of the child. Although the ways of using the Oedipus myth vary widely, a general acceptance of its murky Jocasta symbols runs through the literature. This acceptance is shown by more subtly stated assumptions of a uniquely ambiguous tension existing in the relationship, with damage to sons.

The literature of psychology and sociology in particular is rich in examples. It generally explains the tension in terms of an absent father who has left the wife "as much in need of a husband as the son is of a father." She, therefore, becomes seductive toward the son who in turn projects his own desires and fears unto her. (17) This is even more true in working-class families where the husband presumably is even more absent and the wife, consequently, focuses all of her interest on her son as husband replacement in a baffling way that is both seductive and rejecting. (18)

Such maternal behavior occurs long before the son is of an age to serve as a replacement for the absent husband. A panel report on the psychology of women from the American Psychological Association argues that "there is increasing evidence of distinction between the mother's basic attitudes and handling of her boy and girl children starting from the earliest days and continuing thereafter." (19) While focusing their cross-cultural analysis on feminine role identification, psychologist Whiting and colleagues argue that there exists in infancy an overwhelming mother-son attachment, and they hypothesize that the mother obtains "substitute sexual gratification from nursing and caring for her son." (20)

Sociologist Philip Slater, focusing on the mother-son relationship in the Greek family and Greek mythology in search of parallels for the contemporary American middle-class family, argues that the roots of narcissistic American males are to be found in the overloaded relationship of mother and son. (21) In Greek myths and families as well as contemporary American middle-class culture he posits a threefold interrelationship of sex antagonism, maternal ambivalence, and male narcissism. The binding chain is a sex antagonism that destabilizes the mother's self-concept and hence leads to ambivalent responses to her son, which thus produces male narcissism.

While Slater can be seen as implicitly arguing that the situation may improve with sexual equality, social historian Christopher Lasch finds a mounting tension as women become more equal. Women, says Lasch, have "gained the upper hand ... in the modern middle-class family," intimidating their husbands and, in the process, producing narcissistic and schizophrenic sons. He holds to the theory that "the flawed relations between mothers and their offspring (especially between mothers and sons) hold the key to the psychopathology of our society." (22)

Lasch argues that the American mother as well as the father is an absent parent. This he believes to have happened because: "Outside experts have taken over many of her practical functions, and she often discharges those that remain in a mechanical manner that conforms not to the child's needs but to a preconceived ideal of motherhood."

The consequences for narcissistic sons of women's dominance in the family, as Lasch sees it, are positively awful: "Their unconscious impressions of the mother are so overblown and so heavily influenced by aggressive impulses and the quality of her care so little attuned to the child's needs, that she appears in the child's fantasies as a devouring bird, a vagina full of teeth." (23)

While Slater locates the source of the alleged mother-son tension in the American middle-class family in what he calls the "desexualized" suburban matron, masculine in style because she has been deprived of a meaningful career, Lasch, writing seven years later well into the "sexual revolution," locates the source in what he calls the new narcissistic woman. (24) Her "increasingly insistent demand for sexual fulfillment" he insists, terrifies men with anxieties which "reverberate at . . . deep layers of the masculine mind, calling up early fantasies of a possessive, suffocating, devouring, and castrating mother." (25)

The collective wisdom of the social scientists reflects the cultural imperatives of patriarchal societies that assign responsibility for the nurturing of children to one family member, the mother. Rarely in the literature is the assignment of responsibility itself questioned. Rather, the "overwhelming attachment" between mothers and sons, whether explained or not, is considered to be a given, a necessary evil in the lives of men with often dire consequences. The "compelling power of fate" in the story has served the experts well, even, as we shall see, when the "data" to support the theory do not exist.

PATHOLOGICAL IMPLICATIONS

As *the* responsible one, the mother, at least until very recently, was inevitably to blame for her son's problems. When the "Boston Strangler" was at large torturing women several years ago a medical-psychiatric committee was formed by the stymied police to put together an imaginative detailed profile of the killer. What actually emerged from the committee was an imaginative profile of his mother.

Struck by the advanced age of the first victims, one of whom was 75, the committee postulated . . . that the elusive killer was a neat, punctual, conservatively dressed, possibly middle-aged, probably impotent, probably homosexual fellow who was consumed by raging hatred for his "sweet, orderly, neat, compulsive, seductive, punitive, overwhelming" mother. . . . Consumed by mother hatred, the psychiatrist divined, the Strangler had chosen to murder and mutilate old women in a manner "both sadistic and loving." (26)

We have for examples of the pathological implications of the mother-son relationship the three most heavily researched areas of "social deviation": sons suffering from mental illness; sons who are homosexuals; and sons who are juvenile delinquents. The mother, irrespective of age, class, ethnic, racial, psychological, or genetic considerations, is almost always thought to be responsible. Only very recently have conclusions about the pathological implications of the mother-son relationship begun to change. Ever so slowly, however, this seems to be more a result of crises in the fields of psychoanalysis and psychology than of efforts to reexamine the conventional wisdom as to the mothering role. Political as well as professional forces may be at work. In this conservative era, typically, government research dollars are going to genetic and biological studies more than psychological or sociological ones. The flux of interpretations has left consumers caught in another nature versus nurture controversy, one which includes, of course, puzzled mothers of sons.

To take mental illness first, among psychologists ever since the early 1930s, much attention has been focused on the alleged pathological personalities of mothers of schizophrenic patients, particularly males. (27) The "schizophrenogenic mother" is described as being dominating, cold, over-protecting, and rejecting while at the same time seeking to foster in her son extreme dependency upon her. (28) She is married to a man who is "irrational, passive, withdrawn, unsure of his masculinity, and in need of his wife's admiration." (29)

This mother is held to be the "cause" of schizophrenia (the collective name for many mental diseases) in her son because she is unable to form boundaries between herself and him:

This type of mother seeks compensation for her dissatisfactions with life and the burdens of being a woman by finding completion through a son. She expects little from men whom she considers as weak figures dependent upon their wives or mothers. . . . She manages to be impervious to the needs and wishes of other family members if they do not fit her preconceptions of how things should be. . . . She envisions and seeks to establish a very special relatedness between herself and her son through which her dormant and frustrated potentialities will flow into her offspring. . . . She commonly projects her own insecurities onto the child and becomes overprotective of him. . . . The mother's use of a son in place of her husband as the major source of emotional gratification, which frequently includes highly eroticized and seductive behavior, confuses the oedipal transition. (30)

The way in which this mother deviantly communicates with her son, known as the double bind theory, is the focus of much of the literature on the causes of schizophrenia. (31) The theory holds that schizophrenia is a predictable appropriate response to mixed messages. The mother gives simultaneously at least two orders of message: (1) "hostile or withdrawing behavior which is aroused whenever the child approaches her"; and (2) "simulated loving or approaching behavior which is aroused when the child responds to her hostile and withdrawing behavior, as a way of denying that she is withdrawing." The child, in the most important relationship in his life, "is punished if he indicates love and affection and punished if he does not; and his escape routes from the situation, such as gaining support from others, are cut off." (32)

This schizophrenogenic mother with her double bind behavior remains a popular hypothesis as to the etiology of schizophrenic males. As with most psychoanalytic theories of late, however, increasing numbers of researchers are questioning the objectivity of the data on which the hypothesis rests. They are turning toward causal theories that focus on the genes held to transmit a particular biochemical state that leads to deviant behavior. Such researchers find *no evidence* that double bind communication has greater prevalence in families of schizophrenics; (33) or that maternal dominance in families of schizophrenics is more prevalent; (34) or, finally, that mothers' personalities, communication problems, or inability to break family boundaries causes schizophrenia. (35) While acknowledging that family conflict may act as a "general stress" in the lives of schizophrenics, revisionists conclude that

Many families, with and without a disordered member, give contradictory messages, have one dominant parent, and have family members who find it hard to disengage from the family sphere. Further, many families having a schizophrenic member show none of the deviations and styles of interaction that had been thought to characterize the schizophrenic family. (36)

Beyond the mental health of sons, mothers have long been held responsible for their sexual behavior. The classic psychoanalytic explanation of sexual "deviancy" is:

> Boys who have had too intense and exclusive a relationship with mother in
> early life, exacerbated by an unsympathetic condemnatory father, tend to
> develop particularly strong Oedipal fears. A common manifestation of this in
> adult males is the inability to perform sexually except with prostitutes. Nice
> women are too like mother, hence forbidden fruit, pure and untouchable.
> Homosexual males go one stage further and become cold towards all women,
> because any kind of heterosexual feeling arouses their incest guilt. (37)

Again, until very recently, in almost all studies of the causes of
homosexuality, primacy has been placed on *the voiceless mother*. She is
described as dominating and possessive, both overly restrictive and
overly indulgent. She is married, but, of course, to weak, detached Mr.
Milquetoast for whom her son serves as replaced love object. (38) Of all
the guilt-inducing accusations placed on mothers of sons probably this
one, the making of a homosexual, is the most generally accepted by
everyone and, by mothers, the most widely feared.

As with schizophrenia, there is increasing division among the ranks
of the homosexuality researchers. They are similarly reexamining the
"data" and finding again *no evidence* that male homosexuals more than
heterosexuals recollect being overindulged and overprotected by mothers;
that there exists any significant differences in parental backgrounds
between nonneurotic homosexuals and nonneurotic heterosexuals; or that
family relationships have anything to do with later sexual orientation. It is
argued, in fact, that certain family constellations are a consequence of the
son's effect upon the family rather than vice versa. (39)

In line with developments in schizophrenia studies, the specter of
genetic determinism raises its head in the current etiology of
homosexuality. Zoologist E. O. Wilson argues that homosexuality is
common in other animals and, therefore, human homosexuality may be
an innate, and genetically influenced, condition. (40) A recent report from
the Kinsey Institute for Sex Research at Indiana University tentatively
supports Wilson's hypothesis by concluding that the role of parental
influence has been "grossly exaggerated." The Kinsey researchers find
the mother-son relationship "hardly worth mentioning," suggesting
instead that a predisposition for homosexuality may be set before
birth. (41)

When it comes to the etiology of juvenile delinquency the finger of
the expert points to the mother again, but with several differences among
studies focusing on psychological or sexual problems. First, there is

more consideration of defective fathering beyond absence, including criminality, alcoholism, and neglect. (42) Second, rather than the usual characterization of the defective mother as one who is overprotective, dominating, and seductive with her son, and incapable of a satisfactory marital relationship, here the verdict becomes too much "hands off" rather than too much "hands on." (43) The emphasis is on the rejecting mother (usually because of employment) rather than on the smothering one.

The third difference in explanations of juvenile delinquency compared with those for schizophrenia and homosexuality is that there seems to be less interest in genetic factors. (44) Perhaps this is because most research on juvenile delinquency centers on the urban lower-class subjects who are most likely to be arrested, convicted and incarcerated, and least likely to be sufficiently rich or "fringed" to seek treatment at research centers where genetic factors might be assessed.

Still, the mother is to blame. It is among the urban lower classes, of course, that we find the highest percentages of households headed by females employed in low-salary, low-satisfaction, and low-security jobs. One study argues that the mere fact of coming from a female-headed household leads boys to be "hypermasculine" and, therefore, more likely to become delinquent. It supports the thesis of Talcott Parsons that "the mother-based home generates problems of compulsive masculinity which in turn promote antisocial conduct." (45) Despite acknowledgments that the mother of the juvenile delinquent son faces deprivations herself, primary responsibility for the delinquency remains with her. (46)

Although in general there appears to be a swing away from mother-blaming as the quintessential factor in the social deviation of sons, social scientists still focus on the damage the all-powerful mother does to sons. They continue to portray mothers of sons as psychologically isolated beings capable of enormous destruction (and, theoretically at least, perfection). The *awesomeness* of the responsibility accorded mothers for sons has rarely concerned social scientists. Such silence smacks of the irrational unless we assume that such questioning has been viewed consciously or unconsciously not in the interests of largely male or male-trained researchers, or outside the boundaries of the natural order of human development. This silence provides the foundation for the belief that mothers "cause" schizophrenia, homosexuality, juvenile delinquency, and a host of other social "problems."

To attribute to women this omnipotent power, however, is to deny them their humanity. As a coauthored feminist study recently put it:

Insofar as we treat mothers as larger than life, omnipotent, all-powerful, or powerless . . . we deny mothers the complexity of their lives, their selfhood, their agency in creating from institutional context and experienced feelings. We deny them their place in a two-way relationship with their children, manifold relationships with the rest of the world; and we deny ourselves as mothers. (47)

FEMINISTS SPEAKING OUT

Especially since the 1970s feminists have been challenging the sagacity of the assignment of responsibility for the raising of sons and daughters to mothers alone. (48) They see the glorification of the mothering role as an instrument of women's oppression. They call for the right not to mother, document the darker sides of the mothering experience, and advocate a more equitable sharing of child raising. They argue that the institution of motherhood as currently defined is harmful to both sons and daughters, and mothers themselves.

There is a burgeoning theoretical literature on women's role in the home. From a variety of theoretical and experiential perspectives feminist scholars analyze the inequities of home labor, the changing Euro-American family, the mother-daughter relationship, and the institution of motherhood in general. Marxist and socialist feminists, in particular, show how capitalism combined with patriarchy make both home labor and market labor gender specific, with women's status both economically and psychologically disadvantageous. They argue that most women's work, including child care, as presently carried on in home and market helps perpetuate male domination and the capitalist form of production. Thanks to their analyses we have come to appreciate the connection of mothers to the political economy with heightened sensitivity to class variations of tasks and values. (49)

Surprisingly, however, feminists like the social scientists discussed above have had remarkably little to say about the mother-son relationship from mothers' perspectives. There have been only two feminist books specifically focusing on the mother-son relationship in the past decade: Judith Arcana's *Every Mother's Son;* and Carole Klein's *Mothers and Sons*. Arcana, focusing on the experiences of mothers of young sons, seeks to answer the question: How can mothers raise nonsexist sons? Klein's study is based largely on the views of men. In addition, Jane Lazarre"s *The Mother Knot* gives us a poignant account of the birth of her first son and her mothering experiences of his first two and a half years; and Adrienne Rich shares her ambivalence as mother of two sons in *Of Woman Born.*

By and large, the mother-son relationship does not seem to be a topic many of us choose. Even I do not speak often about my sons and I have noticed my feminist friends and colleagues do not either. It is strange because we speak of almost everything else these days — husbands, lovers, fathers, and especially daughters and our own mothers. We seem to lack "a central firmness and clarity of vantage," that special quality John Updike ascribes to Colette, when it comes to sons. (50) That this is so is but another reflection of the pervasiveness of the murky Jocasta myth. Even we feminists have been silenced by it. Therefore, with this paucity of feminist studies specifically focusing on the mother-son relationship, those on the institution of motherhood in general are what we must build upon.

One of the first contemporary feminists to analyze the experience of mothering is Simone de Beauvoir. With the publication of *The Second Sex* in 1949, she bends feminist theory toward postulating woman as "the other," as second, as lesser. Her conclusions are deeply influenced by the philosophy of existentialism, as propounded by her lifelong companion, Jean-Paul Sartre.

Existentialism was at the height of its vogue while Beauvoir was writing *The Second Sex.* Its details need not detain us, but, briefly, it postulates that human "reality" identifies and defines itself by the ends it pursues. (51) Existentialists argue that people seek to find meaning in life (in the "immanent") through a willful exercise called "transcendence." Within the ethical system of existentialism, human beings could have authenticity only through transcendence.

> Every subject plays his part as such specifically through exploits or projects that serve as a mode of transcendence; he achieves liberty only through a continual reaching out toward other liberties. There is no justification for present existence other than its expansion into an indefinitely open future. Every time transcendence falls back into immanence, stagnation, there is a degradation of existence in the "*en-soi*" — the brutish life of subjugation to given conditions — and of liberty into constraint and contingence. (52)

Beauvoir finds the institution of motherhood to be oppressive and unjust; thus, immanent rather than transcendent. She portrays the great responsibility placed upon mothers as dangerous to children because women, held in a position inferior to men, are almost always discontented. Since they feel less than, that is, inferior, to men they compensate for the frustrations of their lesser station through their children, reaching to them more often than not with sadistic cruelty or with masochistic devotion. She finds it "outrageously paradoxical" that mothers should have prime responsibility for the molding of human beings while being excluded from all meaningful public activities, forced to live lives of mere immanence rather than transcendence.

Women, because of their situation as the "other," are understandably ambivalent about masculine transcendence, Beauvoir argues. Thus, they find the mothering of sons at once both more difficult and more satisfying than the mothering of daughters. Beauvoir realizes that women's mothering experience with both sexes must be viewed within women's total situation. She wants full account to be taken of their family origin, their economic position, their relationship with their husbands, and, importantly, their relationship with themselves. So seen, the mothering of daughters, compared to sons, is clearly different. Mothers' relationships with children of their own sex, she argues, are generally more emotional because with daughters they can more fully reproduce themselves. But fatefully this also reproduces many conflicts with themselves, a situation that is greatly aggravated as their daughters seek independence from them.

According to Beauvoir, mothers want to possess their sons in a different way. They long to keep them within the immanent reality of repetitive familial existence. At the same time they wish to engender heroes, sons who will transcend and through whom they mistakenly hope to transcend themselves. The latter dream is a delusion and women's task is thankless because sons invariably leave their mothers for a world women cannot know.

Although Beauvoir's perception of the mothering experience is obviously after more than three decades of great change quite dated, *The Second Sex* remains an essential point of departure for us. Her central thesis, that women cannot find transcendence, that is, fulfillment, through the mothering of sons, will be recognized as a pervasive theme of the mothers interviewed for this study. So, too, is her contention that the responsibility for the well-being of children placed on mothers is part of their oppression.

Beyond the influential work of Simone de Beauvoir, several other widely read feminist analyses of women's situation are of significance. Betty Friedan's *Feminine Mystique*, published in 1963, is said to have unleashed the contemporary women's movement. Friedan effectively translates Beauvoir's existential discourse into the language of the suburban American housewife of the 1950s. What Beauvoir calls "immanence," she calls "the problem that has no name." She, too, challenges the conventional (and convenient) belief that women can find fulfillment or meaning in life as wives and mothers.

Basing her case on earlier studies by David Levy and Arnold H. Green, Friedan concludes that mothers with thwarted career ambitions almost invariably "smother" both their sons and their daughters. Striking a major theme, she wonders why American culture is concerned primarily with neuroses of smothered sons, not of daughters. She theorizes that females are supposed to be less than fully developed, blocked at an emotional level that recognizes only a need for love. Cultural expectations imposed on daughters keep them infantile; their mothers' smothering therefore is not held to be harmful. Like their mothers, daughters are programmed for "noncommitment" and "vicarious living."

For their sons, Friedan continues, mothers are expected to have great expectations. But through both sons and daughters, she concludes, mothers living vicariously end up dehumanizing their offspring as well as themselves. Expectations placed on sons have a further price. She finds a preponderance of boys among child patients at suburban mental health clinics, along with a preponderance of housewives among adult patients.

In *The Future of Motherhood* sociologist Jesse Bernard uses a functionalist perspective to explore the experiences of mothers. She examines motherhood, after the fashion of a functionalist, as an institution. Like all institutions, Bernard argues, motherhood serves to organize human behavior in prescribed ways deemed socially desirable for given times and places. The basic function of motherhood in modern affluent American society has been to protect and nurture children. Related to this function, she suggests, have been two requirements for mothers: first, full-time care of children; and, second, sole responsibility for their well-being. Bernard sees these functions of motherhood as causing a separation between the roles of women as mothers and as productive workers, a separation unique to the United States.

Writing in the mid-seventies, Bernard believes that technological changes in our society are mandating a change in this functionalist script for mothers. And none too soon, in her opinion. "The terrible weight of responsibility" placed upon mothers has resulted in "structural defects." Anxiety and guilt beset mothers as they frantically attempt to assess their lives by ill-defined, always changing, yet highly idealized standards. While centering on mothers of both sons and daughters, she argues that the defect of institutionalized motherhood is especially damaging to sons.

Their emancipation from maternal overinvolvement is almost always a more intense experience than that of daughters.

Taken together the works of Beauvoir, Friedan, and Bernard suggest a developing line of argument. They question the sagacity of the assignment of solitary responsibility for "mothering" to mothers. They find it harmful to children of both sexes but especially sons. They are also sensitive to the damage done to mothers. The very limitations of opportunities and rewards for women because they are female are the primary source of this tension.

THE PSYCHOLOGY OF WOMEN

Although feminists since Beauvoir have been attacking psychoanalytic interpretations of motherhood with Sigmund Freud at the top of the enemy list, there has been a recent theoretical shift. In fact, psychoanalytic explanations of the personality development of women currently appear to be prevailing over sociopolitical and cultural ones. (53)

Psychologist Dorothy Dinnerstein combines the Freudian and Gestalt visions of societal processes. (54) She attributes to Freud the genius of recognizing as one of the "central defects in human life" the role of women as primary parent in infancy and early childhood. Dinnerstein agrees with Freud that this places an enormous burden on the personality formation of both women and men. What she circuitously challenges in Gestalt fashion is Freud's assumption of the unchangeability of this condition. "Our sexual arrangements," she argues, "are used to keep unresolved a core ambivalence that centers upon our species' most characteristic, vital, and dangerous gift: our gift for enterprise, for self-creation." (55)

The more immediate source of tension between mother and son, for Dinnerstein, derives from the son's (and to a lesser extent the daughter's) difficulty in grasping "the fact of the mother's separate human subjectivity." (56) She is seen as "naturally fit to nurture other people's individuality; as the born audience in whose awareness other people's subjective existence can be mirrored; as the being so peculiarly needed to confirm other people's worth, power, significance that if she fails to render them this service she is a monster, anomalous and useless." And, at the same time, she is also seen "as the one who will not let other people be, the one who beckons her loved ones back from selfhood, who wants to engulf, dissolve, drown, suffocate them as autonomous persons." (57)

The central issue for Dinnerstein as for the others discussed above is that of maternal responsibility. The mother is considered to be the "indispensable quasi-human supporter," and simultaneously the "deadly quasi-human enemy of the self." Not until the primary parent is as much male as female will there be real hope for the human condition. Such hope, according to Dinnerstein, necessitates victory in "our ongoing struggles against our own infantilism, our own struggle to carve out, and fence around, *a realm for the exercise of sober self-reliance.*" Not until then will the mother's human frailties be no longer "at bottom less humanly acceptable than the father's." (58) Unfortunately, Dinnerstein's use of the powerful symbols of Freudian mythology leaves us less than convinced that the "human condition" can be so changed.

Through psychoanalytic lens, sociologist Nancy Chodorow (59) argues that it is the reinforcement of gender differences by mothers that is at the heart of the war between the sexes. (Gender differences are determined primarily by social and cultural phenomena whereas sex differences are physiological phenomena.) She regards women, for psychologically as well as sociologically conditioned reasons, as the pivotal actors in the reproduction process that makes for masculinity. Women's own gender-differentiated personalities lead them to reproduce children with gender-differentiated personalities. She shares the psychoanalytic consensus that infants develop their sense of self mainly in relation to their mothers. But, because mothers differ in gender from their sons, they tend to experience their sons as separate from themselves, as others.

Women reproduce boys who grow away from them, have difficulty relating to others, and participate more easily in the public sphere than the domestic sphere. "A mother . . . may push her son out of his preoedipal relationship [before the age of three] to her into an oedipally toned relationship defined by its sexuality and gender distinction." (60) Because mothers tend to treat their sons as opposites from a very early age and because sons must later repress their attachment to their mothers, sons become adults who experience themselves less in relation to others than do daughters.

According to Chodorow women raise girls who do not grow away from them; girls who become women who remain in the domestic sphere, and spend their lives "mothering" in one way or another. Because mothers experience their daughters in a more symbiotic way, as extensions of themselves, their daughters emerge with a basis for empathy built into their definition of self. They are more nurturing, less differentiated, more preoccupied with relationships than are boys. She insists that for psychological as well as sociological reasons, motherhood has built into it a mechanism for reproducing mothering girls and nonmothering boys.

This psychoanalytic account of the formation of gender identity has broad social implications. Chodorow seems to be arguing that this perpetuation of the mothering process explains male domination itself. (61) A key Chodorow passage makes this clear:

> We can define and articulate certain broad universal sexual asymmetries in the social organization of gender generated by women's mothering. Women's mothering determines women's primary location in the domestic sphere and creates a basis for the structural differentiation of domestic and public spheres. But these spheres operate hierarchically. Kinship rules organize claims of men on domestic units, and men dominate kinship. Culturally and politically, the public sphere dominates the domestic, and hence men dominate women. (62)

Few of the mothers I have encountered while teaching and interviewing could relate to Chodorow's book. As with most psychoanalytic theories her arguments rest on analysts' reconstructions of upper-class patients' reconstructions of their pre-oedipal and oedipal memories. The experiences of mothers of sons of many classes are not part of Chodorow's data. The human element in all its complexity and variation is missing.

Nevertheless, Chodorow's *Reproduction of Mothering* makes an important contribution to the theory of gender personality. It raises some interesting questions for our exploration of the mother-son relationship, ones upon which we must reflect as we attempt to understand the perspectives of the women whose stories follow this chapter. Do mothers of sons for psychological as well as sociological reasons strongly perceive their sons as sexual "others"? Do they, by the very way in which they raise sons, foster a masculinity that in turn fosters sexism? If so, are they, as the makers of men, to be blamed for their own oppression? Finally, if all this follows from Chodorow's gender identity, what is to be done?

The hypothesis that mothers, and all women, are psychologically different from men in a fundamental way appears to be developing into one of the major assumptions of current feminist scholarship. The nub of the psychological difference lies in the self-definitions of the two sexes and those preponderating in the culture. Women define themselves and are defined by others in terms of their relationships with others; men do not similarly define themselves and are not so defined by others. This recurrent observation that is on the way to becoming an assumption has historically a feeling of circularity. It seems to reconstruct the pedestal that feminists have so trenchantly criticized, the celebration of traditional female values.

Carol Gilligan, for example, is one of a growing number of feminists who attempts to put traditional female values in a different context, to center around a caring for others in a noncompulsive way. (63) She sees such caring not just as female but as an essential trait for human development, since human life is impossible without connections to others. Gilligan regards the nurturing traits so frequently associated with mothers as strengths rather than weaknesses. She challenges developmental theorists such as Freud, Erikson, and Kholberg who equate independence and separateness with maturing and thus by unavoidable inference with a higher state of human morality. Women, she argues, tend to recognize the reality of interdependence and connectedness. They have a greater sensitivity than men to moral shading, to ambiguities and uncertainties in human life that cannot be reduced as it were to a mathematical equation of rights and wrongs. Women see a world of many hues and men do not.

With her *In a Different Voice,* a study of how women and men make moral decisions, Gilligan argues that men see themselves in terms of relationships too, but of a different sort. Men view relationships primarily in terms of an abstract code of justice.

Gilligan is working toward a theory of human development that will no longer view women as morally deficient and stunted in growth. Such a theory may well help end the denigration of women because they are sensitive to and caring of others — that is, in the context of this book, because they are "good mothers." The thrust of the theory emerges in her idea that females simply speak "in a different voice" from men, a caring, and thus for any humane society, an essential voice.

Gilligan accepts Chodorow's thesis that mothers mother the way they do for psychologically as well as socially conditioned reasons, that is, that they are the products as well as the producers of gender-differentiated personalities. She, like Chodorow, raises some troublesome questions for our understanding of the mother-son relationship. She, too, invites us to conclude that it is the way mothers see their relationships with their sons from the start that *causes* their sons to speak "in a different voice," one set apart from their own and their daughters. If this is so, is it now to be considered to be mothers' responsibility somehow to teach their sons to speak in a voice the same as theirs? Might this not amount to but one additional ingredient in the already awesome assignment of responsibility of mothers to sons? Might we not be placing mothers of sons, once again, in the all powerful, idolizing/blaming, madonna/whore, irretrievably catch-22 situation?

Such questions are hard and, in the context of present-day life, soul searching. As such they well accord with the evolution of feminist theory. The hesitations and fears that beset the development of feminist theory reflect its special complexity. As Sheila Rowbotham says:

> Thinking is difficult when the words are not your own. Borrowed concepts are like passed-down clothes: they fit badly and do not give confidence; we lumber awkwardly about in them. . . . First there is the paralysis. Their words stick in your throat. . . . There is not only the paralysis, there is the labour of making connections. Theory . . . makes reality intelligible. But this theory is constructed from the experience of the dominators and consequently reflects the world from their point of view. They, however, present it as the summation of the world as it is. (64)

Thinking is particularly difficult when it comes to the mother-son relationship with all its myth-laden baggage. For we who are engaged in seeking an understanding of the experiences of mothers of sons the implications of this recent shift in feminist theory on mothering toward a paradigm that posits women as psychologically different from men in fundamental ways cannot be ignored. This is not to suggest that the feminists just discussed have been unmindful of the enormity of the responsibility already placed on mothers. They have shared with all participants in feminist theory-making the desire to understand and articulate the sources of women's inequality. Nor is it to suggest that they are unaware that women's responsibility for mothering has long been a major source of oppression whatever enhancement of responsibility their theories may imply.

It *is,* however, to suggest that the shifting paradigm reflects an emerging consensus that mothers of sons do have the power to make nonsexist sons. This implicitly places the blame for sexism on mothers who fail to make such men. Desirable as the making of nonsexist men may be, this leaves the blame, in a paradox that must be faced, with unregenerated moms; thus further complicating what is already an impossible assignment. The assumptions underlying this new feminist paradigm come dangerously close to the reification of mothers of sons embedded in the conventional wisdom of the social scientists.

Surely the time has come for mothers of sons themselves to speak out. Feminist theory, all theory, can flourish only through a constant interaction with experience. To borrow from Adrienne Rich, feminist theory must be "rooted in the conviction that all women's lives are important." We must accept with her how "to make visible the full meaning of women's experience, to reinterpret knowledge in terms of that experience, is now the most important task of thinking." (65) Mothers of sons need to speak out. They have been closeted for too long.

> Above the laughter, above the miseries, above the clatter of glasses and the cries of children, I hear a voice saying: Isn't there some statement you'd like to make? Anything noted while alive? Anything felt, seen, heard, done? You are here. You're having your turn. Isn't there something you know and nobody else does? . . . What about all the words that were said and all the words that were never said? (66)

NOTES

1. Tillie Olsen, *Silences* (New York: Dell, 1978), p. 6.

2. I take the liberty of lumping together as "social scientists" those scholars whose work has social implications for mothers of sons. This includes sociologists, historians, psychologists, psychoanalysts, anthropologists, philosophers, physicians, and others as well. Because feminist scholars (who obviously fall into the above categories too) are dealt with separately in this chapter, they are not included.

3. Themes in literature contribute to and reenforce the themes of the social scientists. Hamlet's hesitancy to obtain revenge of his father's murder is attributed to the seductive sensuality of the guilty mother: "Let me not think on 't; frailty thy name is woman!" See Ernest Jones, *Hamlet and Oedipus* (New York: Doubleday, 1954). T. S. Eliot writes: "The essential emotion of the play is the feeling of son towards a guilty mother," (quoted in Jones, p. 114). Gertrude Morrel's engulfing relationship with her son Paul, in D. H. Lawrence's *Sons and Lovers* (London: Duckworth, 1913), symbolizes the seductive, devouring mother. When she tells Paul, "I never really had a husband," she is viewed by us all as sinister, corrupting, with her love for her son. And we all know that Alex Portnoy masturbated to impotence because his mother, Sophie, demanded to see what was in the toilet bowl and accused him of eating *chazerai*. Philip Roth, *Portnoy's Complaint* (New York: Bantam Books, 1970). Novelists, playwrights, and poets, as well as social scientists and mothers themselves have had little to say from the mother's perspective.

4. See, for example, Victor D. Sanua, "Sociological Factors in Families of Schizophrenics: A Review of the Literature," *Psychiatry* 24 (1961), p. 247; and Christopher Lasch, *Haven in a Heartless World* (New York: Basic Books, 1977), p. 217.

5. This incident is not described in Sophocles's play but is manifest in other accounts of the myth. See, for example, G. Devereux, "Why Oedipus Killed Laius," *International Journal of Psycho-Analysis* 34 (1953); and Harold Stewart, "Jocasta's Crimes," *International Journal of Psychoanalysis* 42 (1961), pp. 424–30.

6. Robert Coles, *Irony in the Mind's Life: Essay on Novels by James Agee, Elizabeth Bowen, and George Eliot* (New York: New Directions, 1974), p. 2.

7. Sigmund Freud, "The Interpretation of Dreams," in *The Basic Writings of Sigmund Freud,* ed. A. A. Brill (New York: Random House, 1938), p. 308.

8. See, for example, Philip E. Slater, *The Glory of Hera: Greek Mythology and the Greek Family* (Boston: Beacon Press, 1968), p. 33; Immanuel Vellikovsky, *Oedipus and Akhnaton: Myth and History* (New York: Garden City Books, 1952), p. 183.

9. Slater, *Glory of Hera,* p. 33, quoting Sigmund Freud, *A General Introduction to Psychoanalysis* (1920; reprint, New York: Garden City Books, 1952), p. 183.

10. Sigmund Freud, *New Introductory Lectures on Psychoanalysis,* vol. 22 of the *Standard Edition of the Complete Psychological Works* (London: Hogarth Press, 1933), p. 135.

11. See Juliet Mitchell, *Psychoanalysis and Feminism: Freud, Reich, Laing and Women* (New York: Random House, 1974) for a feminist defense of Freud's oedipal theory; and Gilles Deleuze and Felix Guattari, *Anti-Oedipus: Capitalism and Schizophrenia* (New York: Viking Press, 1977) for a multidisciplinary attack on the theory.

12. Freud, "The Interpretation of Dreams," p. 300. Italics are mine.

13. Sophocles, "Oedipus Tyrannus," trans. David Grene, *The Complete Tragedies* (Chicago University Press, 1959), pp. 980–83. These questions are raised in Harold Stewart, "Jocasta's Crimes," *International Journal of Psychoanalysis* 42 (1961), and H. A. Van Der Sterran, "The 'King Oedipus' of Sophocles," *International Journal of Psycho-Analysis* 33 (1952).

14. Norman O. Brown, *Love's Body* (New York: Vintage Books, 1968), p. 81.

15. Ibid., p. 63.

16. Ibid., pp. 66, 67.

17. Grete Bibring, "On the 'Passing of the Oedipus Complex' in a Matriarchal Family Setting," in *Drives, Affects, and Behavior: Essays in Honor of Marie Bonaparte,* ed. R. M. Lowenstein (New York: International Universities Press, 1953).

18. Nancy Bayley and E. S. Schaefer, "Relationships Between Socio-economic Variables and the Behavior of Mothers Toward Young Children," *Journal of Genetic Psychology* 96 (1960), pp. 61–77; and Mirra Komarovsky, *Blue-Collar Marriage* (New York: Random House, 1962).

19. Eleanor Galenson, "Scientific Proceedings — Panel Reports," Panels on the Psychology of Women, Annual Meeting of the American Psychoanalytic Association, *Journal of the American Psychoanalytic Association* 24, no. 1, p. 159. However, Eleanor Macoby and Carol Jacklin in *The Psychology of Sex Differences* (Stanford: Stanford University Press, 1974), find little differential treatment. This issue is discussed at length by Nancy Chodorow in *The Reproduction of Mothering: Psychoanalysis and the Sociology of Gender* (Berkeley: University of California Press, 1978), pp. 92–110. Chodorow's findings are in accord with Galenson.

20.　John W. M. Whiting, "Sorcery, Sin, and the Superego: A Cross-Cultural Study of Some Mechanisms of Social Control," in *Cross-Cultural Approaches: Readings in Comparative Research,* ed. Clellan S. Ford (New Haven: Human Relations Area Files, 1959), p. 150.

21.　Slater, *The Glory of Hera.*

22.　Lasch, *Haven in a Heartless World,* p. 155.

23.　Christopher Lasch, *The Culture of Narcissism* (New York: Warner Books, 1979), p. 301.

24.　Philip E. Slater, *The Pursuit of Loneliness: American Culture at the Breaking Point* (Boston: Beacon Press, 1972), pp. 53–80.

25.　Lasch, *Culture of Narcissism,* pp. 328, 343.

26.　Susan Brownmiller, *Against Our Will: Men, Women and Rape* (New York: Simon and Schuster, 1975), pp. 203–4.

27.　D. M. Levy, "Maternal Overprotection and Rejection," *Arch. Neurol. Psychiat.* 25 (1931), pp. 886–89; J. Kasanin, E. Knight, and P. Sage, "The Parent-Child Relationship in Schizophrenia," *Journal of Mental Disease* 79 (1934), pp. 249–63; H. Witmer, "The Childhood Personality and Parent-Child Relationships of Dementia Praecox and Manic Depressive Patients," *Smith College Studies on Social Work* 4 (1934), 290–377. Note that much of this literature, and all literature on social deviancy, generalizes about the mother-daughter relationship too but the focus is clearly on sons. A detailed analysis of the literature comparing the impact of mothers upon sons and daughters is beyond the scope of this study.

28.　T. Lidz, S. Fleck, and A. Cornelison, "The Mothers of Schizophrenic Patients," in *Schizophrenia and the Family* (New York: International Universities Press, 1965).

29.　Kayla F. Bernheim and Richard R. J. Lewine, *Schizophrenia: Symptoms, Causes, Treatments* (New York: W. W. Norton, 1979), p. 114.

30.　Lidz et al., *Schizophrenia and the Family,* pp. 326–27.

31.　G. Bateson, *Steps to an Ecology of Mind* (New York: Ballantine, 1972); G. Bateson, Don D. Jackson, Jay Haley, and John Weakland, "Toward a Theory of Schizophrenia," in *Beyond the Double Bind,* ed. Milton M. Berger (New York: Brunner/Mazel, 1978).

32.　Bateson et al., "Toward a Theory of Schizophrenia," pp. 15, 18.

33.　Steven R. Hirsch and Julian P. Leff, *Abnormalities in Parents of Schizophrenics* (London: Oxford University Press, 1975), p. 15.

34.　Ibid.

35.　Bernheim and Lewine, *Schizophrenia: Symptoms, Causes, Treatments,* p. 114.

36.　Ibid.

37.　O. Fenichel, *The Psychoanalytic Theory of Neurosis* (London: Kegan Paul, 1945), quoted in D. J. West, *Homosexuality Re-examined* (Minneapolis: University of Minnesota Press, 1977), pp. 85–118.

38.　Irving Bieber et al., *Homosexuality, A Psychoanalytical Study* (New York: Basic Books, 1962); N. L. Thompson et al., "Parent-Child Relationships and Sexual Identity in Male and Female Homosexuals and Heterosexuals," *Journal of Abnormal Psychology* 73 (1973), pp. 201–6; John Hart and Diane Richardson, *The Theory and Practice of Homosexuality* (London: Routledge and Kegan, 1981).

39.   Hart and Richardson, *The Theory and Practice of Homosexuality*.

40.   E. O. Wilson, *Sociobiology: The New Synthesis* (Cambridge, Mass.: Harvard University Press, 1975) and *On Human Nature* (Cambridge, Mass.: Harvard University Press, 1978).

41.   Alan P. Bell, Martin S. Weinberg, and Sue Kiefer Hammersmith, *Sexual Preference: Its Development in Men and Women* (Bloomington: Indiana University Press, 1981).

42.   S. Glueck and E. Glueck, *Unraveling Juvenile Delinquency* (New York: Commonwealth, 1950); J. McCord, W. McCord, and E. Thurber, "Some Effects of Paternal Absence on Male Children," *Journal of Abnormal and Social Psychology* 64 (1962), pp. 361–69; J. McCord and W. McCord, with I. Zola, *Origins of Crime* (New York: Columbia University Press, 1969); R. Andry, "Paternal and Maternal Roles and Delinquency," *Deprivation of Maternal Care* (Geneva, WHO Public Health Papers, no. 14, 1962); R. J. Gelles, *The Violent Home* (Beverly Hills: Sage, 1972).

43.   David M. Levy, "Maternal Overprotection," *Psychiatry* 1 (1938), pp. 561–91, 2 (1939), pp. 99–128; Ralph S. Banay, *Youth in Despair* (New York: Coward-McCann, 1948); Seymour Rubenfeld, *Family of Outcasts: A New Theory of Delinquency* (New York: Free Press, 1965), pp. 239–94.

44.   New computerized technologies such as the Brain Electrical Activity Mapping (BEAM) machine, the Magnetic Resonance Imaging (MRI) machine, the computerized Axial Tomograph (CAT), and the Positron Emission Tomography (PET), which are now permitting researchers to understand the activities of the brain, may change this. With the use of BEAM, a team at Harvard studying sociopathic adolescents with histories of physically abusing others finds that the boys have abnormalities in their frontal lobes. "There's no question that many forms of sociopathic behavior are organically based," states one of the researchers. "Therefore, if we choose, these individuals could be recognized in advance and monitored." Quoted in Laurence Cherry and Rona Cherry, "Another Way of Looking at the Brain," New York *Times Magazine*, June 9, 1985, p. 56.

45.   I. J. Silvermann and S. Dinitz, "Compulsive Masculinity and Delinquency," *Criminology* 11 (1974), pp. 499–515.

46.   Sheldon and Eleanor Glueck, *Family Environment and Delinquency* (London: Routledge & Kegan Paul, 1962).

47.   Nancy Chodorow and Susan Contratto, "The Fantasy of the Perfect Mother," in *Rethinking the Family*, ed. Barrie Thorne and Marilyn Yalom (New York: Longman, 1982), pp. 67–68.

48.   In keeping with the experiential nature of this study "feminists" are those who call themselves feminists. This definition allows for the wide range of positions and recommendations of individuals who believe that women's interests are important and insufficiently represented. Of course most of the feminists discussed in this chapter are also social scientists.

49.   See, for example, Mariarosa Dalla Costa and Selma James, *The Power of Women and the Subversion of the Community* (Bristol, Eng.: Falling Wall Press, 1972); Margaret Benston, "The Political Economy of Women's Liberation," *Monthly Review* 21, no. 4 (September 1969); Lise Vogel, "The Earthly Family," *Radical America* 7, nos. 4 and 5 (July-October 1973); Wally Secombe, "Housework under Capitalism," *New Left Review* no. 83 (January-February 1975); Maxine Molyneux,

"Beyond the Housework Debate," *New Left Review* 116 (July-August 1979); Martha E. Gimenez, "Structuralist Marxism on 'The Woman Question'," *Science and Society* 42, no. 3 (Fall 1978). Also note the following useful surveys of the extensive literature on family history: Lutz K. Berkner, "Recent Research on the History of the Family in Western Europe," *Journal of Marriage and the Family* 35, no. 3 (August 1973); Michael Gordon, ed., *The American Family in Social-Historical Perspective*, 2d ed. (New York: St. Martin's Press, 1978); Rayna Rapp, Ellen Ross, and Renate Bridenthal, "Examining Family History," *Feminist Studies* 5, no. 1 (Spring 1979); Amy Swerdlow, Renate Bridenthal, Joan Kelly, and Phyllis Vine, *Household and Kin: Families in Flux* (New York: Feminist Press and McGraw Hill, 1980); and a special issue of *Daedalus* (Spring 1977) on the family.

50.   Quoted in Carolyn Heilbrun, "Hers," New York *Times,* Feb. 5, 1981, p. c2.

51.   Jean-Paul Sartre, *Existential Psychoanalysis* (Chicago: Henry Regnery, 1969), p. 19.

52.   Simone de Beauvoir, *The Second Sex,* (New York: Random House, 1974), p. xxxiii.

53.   Juliet Mitchell's *Psychoanalysis and Feminism,* was the forerunner.

54.   Dorothy Dinnerstein, *The Mermaid and the Minotaur* (New York: Harper & Row, 1976).

55.   Ibid., p. xii.

56.   Ibid., p. 108

57.   Ibid., p. 112.

58.   Ibid., p. 237.

59.   Chodorow, *Reproduction of Mothering,* pp. 9–10. More specifically, Chodorow is of the "object relations school," and for those unfamiliar with that, as Pauline Bart explains, "the first thing to understand is that people are called objects. Thus when she speaks of female genital object choice, she does not mean what vibrator you prefer, but what gender you prefer sexually." Pauline Bart, "Review of Chodorow's The Reproduction of Mothering," in *Mothering: Essays in Feminist Theory,* ed. Joyce Trebilcot (Totowa, N.J.: Rowan & Allanheld, 1983), p. 152.

60.   Ibid., p. 107.

61.   Iris Marion Young also points this out in "Is Male Gender Identity the Cause of Male Domination?" in Trebilcot, ed., *Mothering,* pp. 129–46.

62.   Chodorow, *Reproduction of Mothering,* pp. 9, 10.

63.   Carol Gilligan, *In A Different Voice* (Cambridge, Mass.: Harvard University Press, 1982). Also note Jean Baker Miller, *Toward a New Psychology of Women* (Boston: Beacon Press, 1976); and Sara Ruddick, "Maternal Thinking," in Trebilcot, ed., *Mothering,* pp. 213–30.

64.   Sheila Rowbotham, "Women's Liberation and the New Politics," in *The Body Politic: Writings from the Women's Liberation Movement in Britain, 1969–72,* ed. M. Wandor (London: Stage I, 1973), pp. 4–6.

65.   Adrienne Rich, *On Lies, Secrets and Silence* (New York: W. W. Norton, 1979), p. 213.

66.   E. Smart, *The Assumption of the Rogues and Rascals* (London: Jonathan Cape and Polyantric Press, 1978), p. 63, as quoted in Oakley, *Subject Woman,* p. 335.

3

THE AWESOME RESPONSIBILITY

It is obvious that we all have character traits which make us less than perfectly parental. What is not faced head-on is the fact that under present conditions woman does not share man's right to have such traits without loss of human stature, and man does not share woman's obligation to work at mastering them, at shielding others from their consequences.

Dorothy Dinnerstein (1)

UNDERSTANDING THE MOTHERING ASSIGNMENT

Children have certain "demands" that must be met. Infants must be fed, diapered, cuddled, played with, talked to, cared for, loved. Children's lives must be preserved and their growth must be fostered so that they become acceptable to future generations. (2) In fact, human beings of whatever age need far more nurturing than they usually get. This is beyond dispute. Nothing is more important than the nurturing of our children, for their sake and the future of the world! What is not beyond dispute, however, is who should be responsible for seeing that the requisite nurturing gets done, and precisely what constitutes effective nurturing in order to promote this preservation and growth.

In contemporary Western societies mothers hold themselves, and are held by others, to have the primary responsibility for the physical, emotional, and social well-being of their children. Mothers are considered to be the appropriate caretakers of both sons and daughters because they are said to possess something called unconditional love. This means they have the ability to give all and want nothing in return. This responsibility also includes gender specific requirements for mothering. Certainly since Freud, it has been the assumed task of mothers to see that their sons separate from them at an early age, identify with their fathers, and develop culturally accepted notions about masculinity.

How mothers themselves view their responsibility for the well-being of their sons and how they assess their efficacy over time is the subject of this chapter. But first, we need to ask ourselves what it means for women to be responsible in this primary way. Responsibility is the act of being answerable or accountable, as for something within one's power, control, or management. Underlying this assignment of responsibility to one person, the mother, is the assumption that the physical, psychological, and social well-being of her children is truly within her power, control, or management — that she is, in a sense, omnipotent. As one male psychotherapist sees it:

> A man can march through an entire lifetime behaving and thinking that it isn't so. He can grow up, build a career, marry and have children, arrange for his mother's funeral, die. And through it all she will always be the most crucial, most dynamic, and most powerfully influential force in his life. (3)

This assignment of primary responsibility to women is what cements together the components of the mothering myth. The myth, one that contemporary feminists have been persuasively exposing for some time as discussed in the previous chapter, is that all normal women want, need, and are physically, psychologically, and materially able to nurture the world's young. The myth persists in the face of overwhelming evidence of maternal unhappiness and incompetence. The responsibility assignment is what puts a zing and the sting of morality into the fantasy. It is what most women believe they should be able to fulfill, but never can.

Mothers themselves, and all of us, find it difficult to examine critically this assignment for several reasons: one relates to popular, deeply held perceptions about women's nature; another to assumptions about the ways in which children grow and develop; and a third to the ill-defined standards by which we measure "good" mothering.

First, with respect to women's nature, mothers are considered to be innately able to provide unconditional love irrespective of reward or even satisfaction. Certainly since the growth of industrial capitalism in the nineteenth century this maternal virtue has been considered to be, and is still considered to be, so much a part of the natural order of things that questioning it was and is sacrilegious. The assignment and acceptance of responsibility for the unconditional loving of children to mothers has contributed to the very definition of women, whether mothers or not, as the caring, supportive, responsible gender. This is particularly so for mothers of sons.

Mother love, according to Freud, is what makes the mother-son relationship "altogether the most perfect, the most free from ambivalence of all human relationships. The relationship between . . . mother and son . . . furnishes the purest examples of unchanging tenderness, undisturbed by egoistic consideration." (4) And even so enlightened a neo-Freudian as Erich Fromm writes: "Motherly love by its very nature is unconditional." It is a difficult task, according to Fromm, one requiring traits that only mothers possess: "unselfishness, the ability to give everything and to want nothing but the happiness of the loved one."

For Fromm, "Mother is the home we come from, she is nature, soil, the ocean." We have only to experience her love passively: "I am loved because I am. There is nothing I have to do in order to be loved — mother's love is unconditional." In contrast, fatherly love is said to be conditional love. "Its principle is 'I love you *because* you fulfill my expectations, because you do your duty, because you are like me.'" (5)

Second, the responsibility of mothers to children is predicated on certain accepted but questionable assumptions about the ways in which children grow and develop that reflect the dominant cultural and psychological thought of any given historical period. As Philippe Aries reminds us, assumptions about childhood change over time and mothers' roles in the lives of their children were not always as we now know them:

> In medieval society the idea of childhood did not exist; this is not to suggest that children were neglected, foresaken or despised. The idea of childhood is not to be confused with affection for children; it corresponds to an awareness of the particular nature of childhood, that particular nature which distinguishes the child from the adult, even the young adult. In medieval society this awareness was lacking. That is why, as soon as the child could live without the constant solicitude of his mother, his nanny or his cradlerocker, he belonged to adult society. (6)

In post-Freudian Western societies the presuppositions for healthy childhood development include an appreciation of the primacy of infancy, the need for early bonding with the mother, unconditional mother love, and the prolongation of infancy to include adolescence (7) and far beyond. (8) The concept of childhood itself has changed dramatically. In fact, as Jesse Bernard has pointed out, we have prolonged dependence upon mothers to such a fantastic degree that grown sons and daughters feel they have the right to "depend" on mothers. (9) In this sense, we are always our mothers' children. Childhood has become a forever stage in that we now have our responsible mothers to blame for life.

For boys, there are additional problematic assumptions about development that mothers theoretically are required to understand and do something about. These include recognition of the incestuous desires of sons to possess mothers, the need for sons to learn to repress these desires, acknowledgment of the inevitable rivalry between fathers and sons, an appreciation of the inevitable struggle for separation from mothers, and the need for sons to ultimately identify with fathers in order to become "normal," heterosexual, productive men.

The third reason why this responsibility concept is as confusing as it is awesome is the lack of a meaningful definition of what it takes to fulfill one's responsibility — what it takes to be a "good" mother. Sociologist Philip Slater says a successful mother-son relationship depends on the degree of intensity of the mother-son bind, a "not-too-little-not-too-much" kind of prescription. (10) D. W. Winnicott, the British child psychiatrist, says that "good enough" mothering is done by those with "natural self-reliance" who are not afraid of their "great responsibility" and realize that "proper care of an infant can only be done from the heart." According to Winnicott, it is not too difficult a task. He tells mothers:

> In the ordinary things you do you are quite naturally doing very important things and the beauty of it is that you do not have to be clever, and you do not even have to think if you do not want to. You may have been hopeless at arithmetic at school. . . . But all this does not matter, and it hasn't anything to do with whether you are a good mother or not. . . . Isn't it strange that such a tremendously important thing should depend so little on exceptional intelligence. (11)

For mothers who have been attacked as a generation of vipers and held responsible for most of the problems in society this is not much to go on. (12) What is a mother to do? Can we expect anything but anxiety and guilt from mothers who attempt to assess their lives by such ill-defined standards as these?

As we have seen in the previous chapter the literature on mothers of sons, excluding that of contemporary feminists, rarely questions the meaning or the wisdom of the assignment of responsibility to mothers of sons. Rather, it focuses on *how* mothers of sons have failed to live up to their responsibility. Now many feminists, too, seem to be focusing on how women have not lived up to their responsibility as mothers of sons, rather than on the wisdom of the responsibility assignment itself. In American academic circles it is Nancy Chodorow's widely quoted cumbrous *Reproduction of Mothering* and Carol Gilligan's seductively appealing *In A Different Voice* that best represent this shifting interest in and consensus on women's responsibility for the mothering of sons.

Many of the women interviewed for this book who have both sons and daughters do acknowledge a certain connectedness (not always enjoyable) with their daughters they do not have with sons. Chodorow is correct in arguing that the ways in which many (though certainly not all) women relate to their daughters serves to perpetuate the institution of motherhood and produce gender differentiated personalities in both sons and daughters. As Adrienne Rich suggests, the cathexis between mothers and daughters may be, indeed, "the great unwritten story."

> Psychic osmosis. Desperate defenses. The power of the bond often denied because it cracks consciousness, threatens at times to lead the daughter back into "those secret chambers . . . becoming like waters poured into one jar, inextricably the same, one with the object one adored." (13)

The problem with Chodorow's and Gilligan's impact is that rather than turning to a questioning of the wisdom of the responsibility itself, feminists are implicitly and explicitly redefining the responsibility. (14) It goes something like this: Mothers have the obligation not only to provide for the physical, emotional, and social well-being of their sons, but also to eliminate gender distinctions and produce nonsexist sons (from a Freudian perspective, a contradiction in terms, of course). As with the conventional wisdom on mothers of sons, this recent feminist scholarship implicitly assumes that mothers are all powerful. It calls on women to assume their rightful responsibility for their children's welfare in order to effect a nonpatriarchal society. (15)

The differences between the traditional and the recently revised feminist approach to the mother-son relationship center on the reasons why mothers mother the way they do, and what it means to be a "good" mother. For these feminists, the "good" mother is she who, in spite of her oppression, assumes the responsibility for raising sons who are physically, emotionally, and socially well adjusted and who do not separate from her, do not identify with their fathers, and do not assume the traditional masculine values! The emerging consensus among feminists appears to be that if only mothers would stop reenforcing gender differences in their sons there would be a world of healthy males and an end to patriarchy. The mothering of sons assignment remains as awesome as ever — in fact, more so.

VOICES FROM MOTHERS

What has been missing from explorations of the mother-son relationship all along is the actual voices of mothers. What on earth is going on in their minds, we must ask ourselves? How do they define their responsibility? And how do they feel they measure up to it? Surely mothers themselves must know, albeit with varying levels of feminist consciousness, that they are not all loving, all powerful, all perfect. What happens to them as they invariably discover they haven't measured up? What are the personal and political consequences for both feminist and nonfeminist mothers and their sons of this assignment of responsibility to mothers alone for the well-being of sons?

As we might expect, almost all of the mothers who participated in this study perceive themselves to have the primary responsibility for the well-being of their sons, a responsibility they find to be enormous and never-ending. (16)

Mother of four sons between the ages of 15 and 28. Who knew? Who knew? I mean, if I knew then what I know now. My God! The responsibility! Thank God you are naive when you are young and you just pump them out because you'd be scared to death if you really knew.

The ways in which the women define this responsibility vary with their age, class, and all the other factors that make up their and all women's total situations.

Black, welfare mother of two sons, 24, 26. They've got to be taught how to survive. That is what I've been trying to get across to them for the past twenty some odd years. That is what motherhood is all about in my opinion.

Working-class mother of two sons, 24 and 25. My major job has been to compensate for what others have done to my sons. That has been my function as a mother as I see it. The speciality of my husband's house, of his entire family, is becoming an alcoholic. I was the one who always had to try to compensate for that so they could at least function.

Upper-class mother of two sons, 13 and 16. I consider my main responsibility is to provide structure for my sons. It started when my oldest son was very young. He was the sort of child that needed to have a very structured atmosphere where meals are on time, where his clothes are neatly placed in his drawers, where the house is quiet when he does his homework. My role, as I see it, is make things go smoothly for both of them.

Upper-class mother of three sons, 15, 21, 22. I feel I must give them a sense of commitment to something. I guess I am a driven person and I like people who have some kind of consuming passionate concern. It really doesn't matter what it is.

The common factor for most of the middle-class women is that they feel responsible for providing an environment where the sons can find "happiness."

Mother of a son, 12. I have to admit that I fall asleep quickly at night only when I know that my son has had a happy day.

Mother of four sons, 18, 22, 25, 27. What I want to give my sons is the ability to be happy with themselves long before their mother was able to be with herself.

Mother of two sons, 19 and 21. I really can't stand it when I talk on the phone to the boys and they don't sound happy. I really go berserk. They know this and they tease me about it. But I just can't stand it when they don't sound happy. Somehow I always think it's my fault.

Precisely what these women mean by "happiness" is not at all clear. (I too say that all I want for my sons is that they be "happy.") Simone de Beauvoir is correct to caution us on the usage of that word. She argues that it is even less clear what true values the term masks. "There is no possibility of measuring the happiness of others, and it is always easy to describe as happy the situation in which one wishes to place them." For the middle classes, she asserts, happiness often means "a gilded mediocrity lacking ambition and passion, aimless days indefinitely repeated, life that slips away gently toward death without questioning its purpose." (17) Given the complexity and enormity of the responsibility of mothering sons, perhaps this comes close to what mothers of sons really do mean.

Irrespective of class differences and the vagueness and variations in their definitions of the responsibility itself, few mothers I have spoken with feel they have measured up. If there is a single dominant theme in the interviews for this study it is mea culpa.

Mother of two sons, 20 and 18 and one daughter, 22. I feel hot with shame when I think of that period when my children were toddlers. I didn't really have the ability to enjoy them. All I remember is this feeling of pressure and tension. I would get up in the morning and my unspoken motive was to get through whatever it was that was necessary to do to them so that I could do something enjoyable for myself. And of course, I would never get through to that. I would be trying to visit with friends and there would always be these faces pushing between. And diapers to be changed and food to be prepared. I still feel the shame. After all, they didn't ask to be born. It's my absolute prime commandment. I tell them that frequently — even now that they are grown up. I do not expect gratitude. They didn't ask to be born. I wanted to have them. And it was my bloody responsibility.

Mother of three sons, 18, 22, 24. It's very difficult to look back and honestly reflect on what you've done because you know you haven't done that great. My whole concept of motherhood was from the movies in the fifties. You got married and lived happily ever after. I could see myself married to someone I really adored, having kids, loving them, taking care of them, seeing them grow up, go to school, get straight A's, go to college, get wonderful jobs, find wonderful spouses, have children, and on and on and on. The American dream. I would just put it all in a machine and crank it out. As a mother of small children, I felt very adequate, but suddenly, when I was faced with adolescence, I hit a real wall. At that point I said "Oh boy, I don't know anything about anything." When the boys hit adolescence everybody went bananas because nothing worked out as I thought it would. Everybody went bananas, especially me!

For many women the issues of gender differentiation complicate the responsibility assignment.

Mother of one son, age 6. Sometimes I wish I had had a daughter. I think it would have been simpler. I think women have a big problem with sons these days. There aren't any valid rules anymore. It's like what do you do with a boy? What do you want him to be like? I mean, it seems like it would be easier to know the direction you wanted to push a girl. I know I'd want her to be independent, adventuresome, strong. I just don't think we know what we want to expect from a boy anymore. We just don't know what our responsibility is anymore.

Mothers have long been held responsible for their son's "deviant" behavior. As discussed in the previous chapter, until very recently in almost all studies on the etiology of mental illness, juvenile delinquency, and homosexuality primacy has been placed on the mother's behavior. The guilt of these women is most poignant. For example, one mother of a son who is gay tells us:

"I have tucked my problem away in a corner. I guess my fear is I might feel responsible and I cannot handle it. I have searched my soul and my life many many sleepless nights to see if it was something I did or did not do. For sure Jim was our first born and we were novices at being parents so I'm sure I made mistakes. God, I am so afraid that someone will say: 'Ah ha! That is it. If you had not done that everything would be fine.' I just cannot handle that right now. Jim was born prematurely (probably cause I smoked — guilt number one). He was in the hospital after his birth for almost three months — wasn't supposed to make it. Then one day they handed him to me (I hadn't been allowed to touch him those three months) and said take him home. I was scared and overprotective, I'm sure. Then, he used to wear my high heels when he was four and Doctor Spock said not to make a big deal of it so I would just quietly say no, you are going to ruin my shoes. Then, when he went to school his teachers told me he was a genius. I didn't know what to do about that. Neither of us are geniuses for sure. Then, after graduation from college he told us he was gay and was moving into his own apartment. He said he had been unhappy and different since he was thirteen years old. This nearly broke my heart to think of him having this problem all by himself for all these years. Of course I had feelings and fears that I did not want to face all this time. Perhaps with never having had a brother and no father around for most of my life I didn't really have the proper experience to be the mother of sons."

UNCONDITIONAL LOVE

It is near blasphemy but it has got to be said. Mothers do not always find their relationships with their sons to be one of "the purest examples of unchanging tenderness, undisturbed by egoistic consideration." They do not feel they have the "unselfishness, the ability to give everything and to want nothing but the happiness of the loved one." Their perception of their inability to provide unconditional love, furthermore, produces destructive guilt.

I have been often surprised at the openness with which mothers eagerly discuss extremely delicate issues involving their personal lives. One of the few taboo subjects for some was questioning of mother love. For several any suggestion of its absence was the darkest secret they had to share. Yet for most, share they did.

My own mother, at the age of 72, feels that when she was a young mother she was not loving enough with my younger brother. It was very difficult for me to interview her whom I had always considered a model nurturer. However, she wanted to tell her story. Although she says she is very content with their relationship now, she still has dreams to remind her of the ways in which she failed her son, my brother. Here is one she recently described to me.

"Your brother and I are on a train. He is about five years old, dressed in a little gray Eton suit with a green sweater underneath. You and your father are not there. Then suddenly we are at a picnic or fair in a large meadow. There are many people around, all in a festive party mood. A man asks me to dance. We dance and dance all night long. As the sun is rising I suddenly remember my son. I dash back to the place where I had left him but he is gone. I run to a Railway Express Office and ask if someone there has found my little boy. The man at the desk says they have found several little boys that night and that their clothes are in this trunk. I frantically search through the contents of the trunk but the little gray Eton suit and the green sweater are not in it. I run from one Railway Express office to another but I never find my son."

My mother told me that she awoke the morning after this particular dream with a splitting headache. She said she didn't know what to make of a dream like this. Not long after it my brother visited her and she told him about it. She feels that might have been a mistake on her part because he responded, in a not quite joking tone: "See I've always said you loved my sister more than you loved me and the dream proves it." That was not true, she protested to me, but then went on to explain:

"That isn't true at all, although, I do remember being extremely disappointed when he was born. The first thought I had when I heard I had delivered a boy was what the hell will I do with him? I had had a sister, I loved having a sister, and I wanted a sister for you. Although I attribute this feeling to the fact that I had no brothers and my wonderful mother dominated our household I still feel very guilty. There was something about his maleness and my not wanting to make a sissy out of him I think."

My brother was born in 1942, several years before Dr. Spock's more permissive approach to the care of infants became fashionable. My mother thinks that this might have been part of her problem, although she readily acknowledges that she did not raise me (born five years earlier) in a similar manner. In fact, she tells me, she never let me cry at all.

"From the moment I brought him home from the hospital I adhered to all the rules of the day regarding when babies should be fed, changed, touched, and fondled. Boy, did I stick to them with him although I could never have stood to let you scream like that. But he would cry and cry in his carriage in the backyard and I felt I just had to let him go. I remember one day an elderly neighbor telephoned to ask me to stop that baby from screaming. He said he already had one foot in the grave and I was putting the other there fast. I was very embarrassed."

She wonders whether if she had held him more frequently "he would not have taken so long to find himself. Perhaps he would not have been such a difficult boy. I don't mean that he was bad. He had troubles in school; he couldn't seem to learn what he should learn and he had speech problems too. This probably didn't have anything to do with my handling of him but I still have these feelings. I didn't know how to relate to him."

She doesn't think my father knew how to "relate" to him either, but she excuses him. "I don't remember him playing ball, going on camping trips, or doing any of those things fathers and sons are supposed to do. However, your father was often away on business and I was home most of the time. I should have been more loving."

My mother assumes responsibility for everything that happens to my brother in adulthood too. However, when she speaks of her relationship with him as an adult the root cause of her inadequacy changes. For example, his divorce:

"In a sense, your brother's divorce was my fault. The big mistake I made for which I take full responsibility was permitting him to marry at nineteen. He was really too young but I liked his girlfriend so much and I had this feeling that she was going to be the answer for him. Everything would be straightened out and he would find life really beautiful with her. That was ridiculous. I was wrong. I should have taken a stand but instead I made everything extremely easy for them, like making an apartment in our home for them while he was finishing college. It wasn't right."

Her self-blaming focus shifts from her relational inadequacies toward her son in his infancy to her over-protecting, coddling tendencies. Her tone changes from one of self-doubting to one of suppressed anger and indignation toward my brother. "Responsibility has to come into the act. Your father and I had responsibilities. We went through the depression. We never had parents who handed things to us on a silver platter, believe me."

The ways in which my mother blames herself for events in my brother's life, most of which were quite clearly beyond her control, are especially representative of the isolated agonies expressed by older, middle-class, full-time "homemakers" in this study. Like the women Betty Friedan had in mind when she wrote the *Feminine Mystique* (the Smith graduating class of 1942), these women I spoke to are not conscious of "the women's problem." Rather, they feel that something is wrong with them. For my mother, she could not love enough.

STAYING IN CONTROL

It is by no means only the mature, full-time homemakers like my mother who suffer (along with their sons) from their unquestioning acceptance of the mothering of sons responsibility. Almost all of the women I spoke to believed they had the power to control the lives of their sons; as my mother did her son's marriage. If only. . . . This should not surprise us since, as we have seen, built into this assignment is the assumption that women have the power and ability to control their sons' lives. A male therapist writes:

> What is communicated . . . is a *whole world* perceived and interpreted by his
> mother: The whens and wheres of pleasure and pain, the identity of the father,
> the good guys and the bad guys, the blacks and the whites and sometimes the
> grays, the fears and securities. All these arbitrated by a mother, like a deity,
> the great goddess, for good or ill. . . . This is power. Ultimate power. (18)

Most of the professional women in this study — those who were, at least on the surface, extraordinarily confident, with a clear, articulated sense of who they were, why they were the way they were, and where they were going — were also unquestioning of the assignment. The inevitable sense of failure is the leitmotif for them too.

Katherine is a 47-year-old divorced hospital administrator, who has raised her son, now 21, alone. She defines herself as "a controlling person," a characteristic she feels has complicated her ability to carry out her responsibility as a mother. "My father was a physician and from the time I was seven I had wanted to be a physician. I am the classic study of the 'managerial woman.' I am oriented toward running my universe, being in control. I'm really confident, utterly confident, and ambitious."

The first mistake she feels she made was to try to be a housewife.

"I knew some women who have this sort of background who are housewives too — the kind who run every volunteer agency in town and manage their houses and run their families with considerable finesse. I guess that is the way I saw myself. I deliberately rejected medicine on the theory that I knew I was going to marry and I felt that kind of commitment would be too much of a burden for the family I planned to raise. However, that decision to have a baby and be a housewife, as it turned out, was one of the biggest mistakes I ever made, a real misconception. It is very clear to me now that I was a professional woman, would be a professional woman, and will die a professional woman."

Katherine says that she was not prepared for the responsibility of motherhood. Nor, does she feel her husband was prepared for fatherhood.

"Both my husband and I were misled by my confusion. I married a man who was exciting, tense, witty, highly verbal, with a lot of neurotic problems. My father always referred to him as my project. He needed a lot of attention and until we had Tommy he had all my attention. I genuinely feel that interjecting an offspring into this situation was one of the factors that caused the divorce. I mean you love an infant differently than you love a husband but if your husband wants to be loved in both ways you have trouble."

When her son was born she describes a year of frenetic activity. "The first year of my son's life was the only year in my adult life that I didn't work. But I was chairman of the Ways and Means Committee of the Elks Auxiliary and I ran the fall craft and gift fair for the University Club and I did some visiting for the American Cancer Association and I went to Church Circle."

Katherine feels the marriage began to fall apart because her husband was threatened by all this activity. "My husband found all this activity very disturbing. He thought of it as a failure within himself that I needed to do all these things."

But she blames herself too. "I regret a lot of things that happened that year. I wasn't home very much. I got involved in an affair because I was so miserable. I was destructive. It was bad. I guess I needed to have the marriage end but it was my husband in the end who insisted on a divorce and he was probably right."

Katherine feels she did not handle the divorce well and her "lack of control" has affected her son.

"I was so wrapped up in the emotional problems of divorce that God knows what I missed in terms of what Tommy was doing. I do believe that Tommy never dealt with the fact that his father really left. As children grow up the problem is that what they understand at two is different from what they understand at four or ten. You have to keep telling the whole story over again and again and it took me a while to realize that. You are not born knowing this sort of thing. It's very painful if you, the mother, don't want to dig up all this sort of garbage for the kid when you've barely covered it over for yourself. Tommy didn't want it dug up. He wanted to deny it. Both of us did."

Katherine believes that because Tommy was never permitted to "work through" his rage over his parents' divorce, he developed "an enormous amount of suppressed rage." This caused him to have problems in school. Katherine, like many mothers in this study, alternates between blaming others such as teachers and herself. For example:

"Tommy was thrown out of a private progressive Quaker school when he was in the third grade. The teacher was a very nice, sweet, passive, typical Quaker lady who turned out to be sick because right after she got through that year I heard she was hospitalized in the psychiatric center. She was clearly mentally ill and that is what was going wrong but the principal took the position that my son was the sick one."

Katherine's view of her contribution to her son's school problems is complex.

"Now I did recognize that Tommy was being obnoxious. But I knew that he knew that the teacher was a loser. Boy, mother learned on that one because I had thought that a semi-permissive atmosphere was a good thing. It is not. It is good only for children who don't need help. Now we are really not talking about Tommy's problem so much as we are talking about mine."

After recognizing the shifting focus of her thoughts, Katherine relates her son's school problems to her deficiencies as a mother.

"Unfortunately I am one of those people who doesn't learn anything intuitively. If it can be written down in a book I can learn it. Being a mother did not come naturally to me. I only know about mothering from those things I have been able to learn in an educational environment. If I could have had a Ph.D. in mothering I would have been fine. I do everything from the cerebral cortex on up. I just don't permit anything to come from underneath. I had to learn explicitly and intellectually what I should do with my child."

She says that Tommy's problems stem from her attempt to suppress her controlling nature, an attempt spurred by her ex-husband's accusations.

"Tommy needed structure and I didn't know that. I didn't want to give him structure because my husband had accused me of having made every major decision in the marriage and I decided I would never attempt to control another human being. Unfortunately that included Tommy and I failed to make demands on him. He needed security of structure and I was not giving it to him. I gradually learned to impose more structure but it was tough. He didn't like the structure."

Katherine relates that she then decided her responsibility as mother was to provide what she calls "a security of structure."

"As mother I have had to take dreams away from him. He had a security blanket and he also had a crib he did not want to give up even when he was too long to sleep in it. I saw to it that the blanket and the crib vanished one summer. I feel I have had to drag this child out of infancy kicking and screaming all the way. His fantasy was and still is: I never want to be more than two years old because when I was two I still had Daddy and Mommy, my blanket and my crib."

She feels that she "gets so urgent" about Tommy's "fantasies" because of the divorce (almost 20 years earlier). "Because of that experience I firmly believe in the importance of being realistic, hard-nosed, even when it hurts. I don't want to pretend that something isn't true when it is. I am committed to finding out what smells and throwing that away."

Even though Tommy is now 21, Katherine still defines her responsibility as destroying Tommy's fantasies.

"Now Tommy doesn't want to hear from me that his girlfriend is bad news. He doesn't want to hear from me that he has to give up his security blanket. He actually said to me: 'It feels so nice when I put my head on her tummy.' I said to him: 'Now listen, for one year of your life — from birth to twelve months — you are entitled to total care. That's it, man. You are never entitled to it again.' My only hope is that this latest security blanket named Lisa vanishes before there is a marriage or a pregnancy."

On a certain level Katherine says she recognizes her controlling impulses and their cost to both her son and herself.

"I do understand that I am enormously potent and that for anybody to grow up in my shadow must be some kind of a problem. I think Tommy has now left me and that is healthy for him. He needs to make his own way. My own brother sat around the house until he was twenty-nine because my father didn't have the guts to throw him out. I'm better than that. In one generation we've made some progress."

She is guardedly optimistic about Tommy's future without her. "I believe that Tommy will come out of it, but not without a crash. I just hope he learns from the crash. My only hope is that this latest security blanket named Lisa vanishes. . . . Somehow he's got to make it on his own. I know that."

The thought of Tommy on his own is not unappealing.

"It's a funny thing. Suddenly I have a kind of sense of freedom, of release. I have spent twenty-one years with him always on my mind. I have been thinking, planning, organizing, and deciding what I should do about whatever the hell he was doing for all these years. All of a sudden I have this package of time and emotional energy."

In a follow-up conversation two years later, however, Katherine says that this new freedom she had envisioned did not materialize. Tommy's girlfriend Lisa was, in fact, pregnant, Tommy did marry her, they now have a child, the marriage is in shambles according to Katherine, and she is desperately trying to convince Tommy to enroll in a nearby university and get out of the marriage.

REFLECTING ON THE RESPONSIBILITY
OF MOTHERS TO SONS

As sincere as we may be in this effort to put understanding and appreciation of the complexity of all human relationships into that between mother and sons, we (men and women, feminists and nonfeminists alike) are ready with our barrages of blame. Even if we've read a hundred pop psychology books telling us how to be nonjudgmental when it comes to mothers of sons we find it an impossible task. This is so because we all, women as well as men, long for the perfect mother. We want someone to be responsible for us.

Our collective nightmare is life without the responsible mother. Joyce Carol Oates, in her idiosyncratic, grotesquely humorous novel, *Expensive People,* captures the horror of it all. She confronts the human limitations of the mother-son relationship head on. Richard Everett, the fat, 18-year-old protagonist, who describes himself as "Hamlet stunted at eleven years of age," killed his mother when he was 11. Unlike most accounts of family violence, especially matricide, Richard did not kill her to be free of her. On the contrary, he yearned for dependence, and matricide was the only conceivable way he felt he could maintain the bond with his mother, Nada.

Nada was no smothering mother, covertly desiring submission and dependence for Richard. She wanted to be free of the responsibility and she made that clear to her son. When Richard called her "mother" instead of "Nada" she scolded:

> I don't particularly care to be called *Mother* by anyone. I don't respond to it. I'm trying to hold my own and that's it. No *Mother,* no *Son.* No depending on anyone else. . . . You're not going to blame me for anything.

"Who should I blame then?" was poor Richard's question to her. "Nobody," was Nada's response.

> There are certain times in a person's life . . . when one simply has to shake himself free. You remember how your little puppy Spark used to shake water off himself? Wasn't that cute? Well, . . . everyone must be free himself of impossible pressures, of restraints and burdens that suffocate him. (19)

We all believe in our heart of hearts that few mothers of sons are Nadas. And certainly our experiential knowledge and the literature on womanhood confirms this. Parenting is different for a man and a woman

— of this there's little doubt. Women's sense of self is importantly connected to the world of interpersonal relationships in ways that men's are not. Mothers are viewed as connections to the internal world, fathers to the external one. Even women who are actively trying to combat the ideology of motherhood find themselves struggling with their own psychology — "counting the gains in their new ways of being, but ever conscious also of the costs, of the conflicts that engage them in both their internal world and the external one." (20)

But to agree that because women's developmental experiences have led them to be generally more relational than men they should therefore be assigned the primary responsibility for the welfare of sons is absurd. To assign total responsibility to one person for another is tantamount to eternal damnation for both. The mother-son relationship is doomed to fail. It is no wonder that social scientists have found it impossible to construct benign accounts of mother-son relationships. No person can successfully be responsible for the meaning of another's being. Not even mothers of sons. As Simone de Beauvoir has wisely counseled:

> Even when the child seems a treasure in the midst of a happy or at least a balanced life, he cannot represent the limits of his mother's horizon. He does not take her out of her immanence; she shapes his flesh, she nourishes him, she takes care of him. But she can never do more than create a situation that only the child himself as an independent being can transcend; when she lays a stake on his future, her transcendence through the universe and time is still by proxy, which is to say that once more she is doomed to dependency. Not only her son's ingratitude, but also his failure will give the lie to all her hopes; as in marriage or love, she leaves it to another to justify her life, when the only authentic course is freely to assume that duty herself. (21)

The blunt message of this chapter, and broadly speaking, the entire book, is that both the conventional themes and the revised feminist view of the responsibility of mothers for sons is personally and politically damaging for both mothers and sons, women and men. To concentrate on how mothers fail to live up to their responsibility when it comes to the raising of sons is to miss the point.

Expectations about mothers and motherhood are slow to change. Many women, particularly those in mid-life, do express their satisfaction in life in terms of how they view the results of their years as mothers as measured by the happiness of their sons. For many women being "the essential one" in the family is a hard role to give up.

Although I believe I have a wholesome relationship with our youngest son who was born shortly before I returned to graduate school and is truly a product of "shared parenting," I have lapses concerning my redefined mothering identity from time to time. One such lapse was the time he at age 12 had an emergency appendectomy. On this particular day I had called from work to "check on things," only to discover my husband had taken our son to the hospital. I dashed from work to the hospital in time to see him being wheeled off to surgery, his hand tightly clutching his father's. After the operation (successful) my husband, who is prone to insomnia and late night hours anyway, said he wanted to stay in our son's room for the night in case he awoke frightened or in pain. This certainly seemed like a sensible decision and I scampered home to bed.

But I could not sleep. Something was wrong. I felt extremely anxious. Surely our son would be expecting me, his mother, to be by his bedside when he awoke, I thought to myself. Not stopping for breakfast I dashed back to the hospital at the crack of dawn, theoretically to relieve my husband but in reality to be "the essential one" for our son.

When I arrived three big tears rolled down our son's cheeks and he said, "Daddy, don't go. I felt so safe with you all night by my side." My body stiffened. For a moment I felt almost an uncontrollable rage toward the child. I wanted to shake his poor sore little form and scream: "I am your mother and you feel safe with only me alone." The irony of it all! Here before my very eyes had been the most beautiful proof that the mothering of sons can be shared and when I am shown not to be the essential one I almost go berserk.

But I and most women are beginning to understand the price that is paid by both mothers and sons when only the mother is the essential one. The silence is broken now. The responsibility assignment is beginning to be questioned. With a daring openness women are reflecting on what it means to fail at a task that is so defined that no one can succeed. They are also talking about the futility of their guilt, their lack of control, their feelings of ambivalence, their anger at the injustice of their situation, and the joy they are finding as they learn to free themselves of it.

As will be seen in the chapter to follow, when mothers discuss their expectations for their sons and for their relationships with them they are questioning their responsibility assignment in unfeigned ways that are rocking the very foundations of our present gender system.

NOTES

1. Dorothy Dinnerstein, *The Mermaid and the Minotaur: Sexual Arrangements and Human Malaise* (New York: Harper & Row, 1977), pp. 237, 238.

2. See Sara Ruddick, "Maternal Thinking," in *Rethinking the Family,* ed. Barrie Thorne and Marilyn Yalom (New York: Longman, 1982), pp. 76–94, for an excellent portrayal of the daily practices of mothering. If proof be needed that people past childhood need nurturing, it is estimated that 2.4 million youths in the United States (15 percent of all teenagers between 16 and 19) are so alienated from society that they are unlikely to become productive adults. Binghamton *Press and Sun-Bulletin,* Nov. 2, 1985, p. 1A.

3. Paul Olsen, *Sons and Mothers* (New York: Fawcett Crest, 1981), pp. 21, 22.

4. Sigmund Freud, *New Introductory Lectures on Psychoanalysis,* ed. and trans. James Strachey (New York: Norton, 1961), p. 133; *A General Introduction to Psychoanalysis,* trans. Joan Riviere (New York: Garden City Publishing, 1943), p. 183.

5. Erich Fromm, *The Art of Loving* (New York: Perennial, 1974), pp. 33, 35, 36, 43.

6. Philippe Aries, *Centuries of Childhood* (New York: Knopf, 1963), p. 128.

7. G. Stanley Hall, *Adolescence: Its Psychology and Its Relations to Physiology, Anthropology, Sociology, Sex, Crime, Religion and Education* (New York: Appleton, 1904), 2 vols.

8. Kenneth Keniston, *The Uncommitted: Alienated Youth in American Society* (New York: Dell, 1960).

9. Jesse Bernard, *The Future of Motherhood* (New York: Penguin Books, 1974).

10. Philip Slater, *The Glory of Hera: Greek Mythology and the Greek Family* (Boston: Beacon Press, 1968).

11. D. W. Winnicott, *The Child, The Family, and the Outside World* (Middlesex, Eng.: Harmondsworth, 1961), pp. 16, 105.

12. Philip Wylie, *Generation of Vipers* (New York: Farrar & Rinehart, 1942).

13. Adrienne Rich, *Of Woman Born* (New York: W. W. Norton, 1976), p. 225; and, quoting Virginia Woolfe, p. 231 from *To the Lighthouse* (New York: Harcourt, Brace, 1927), p. 79.

14. Among the feminists who argue positions similar to that of Chodorow viz., the power of mothers are Judith Arcana, Dorothy Dinnerstein, Lilian Rubin, Carol Gilligan, and Adrienne Rich. Interestingly, Chodorow herself is extremely sensitive to the dangers of "mother-blaming" in Chodorow and Susan Contratto, "The Fantasy of the Perfect Mother," in *Rethinking the Family,* ed. Thorne and Yalom, pp. 54–75.

15. Germaine Greer states: "We have at least to consider the possibility that a successful matriarch might well pity Western feminists for having been duped into futile competition with men in exchange for the companionship and love of children. . . ." *Sex and Destiny: The Politics of Human Fertility* (New York: Harper & Row, 1984), p. 29.

16. Only four of the women interviewed felt they did not have primary nurturing responsibility.

17. Simone de Beauvoir, *Second Sex* (New York: Random House, 1974), pp. xxxiii, 500.

18.   Olsen, *Sons and Mothers*, p. 14.

19.   Joyce Carol Oates, *Expensive People* (New York: Vanguard, 1968), pp. 213, 225, 110, 111.

20.   Lillian B. Rubin, *Intimate Strangers* (New York: Harper & Row, 1983), p. 187.

21.   Beauvoir, *Second Sex*, p. 585.

4

EXPECTATIONS

A son will be a leader of men, a soldier, a creator; he will bend the world to his will, and his mother will share his immortal fame; he will give her the houses she has not constructed, the lands she has not explored, the books she has not read.

Simone de Beauvoir (1)

THE MALE PERSPECTIVE ON MOTHERS' EXPECTATIONS

"What does she *want* from me?" sons never stop asking. Mothers' expectations for their sons are thought to be different from all other earthly ones. As many men see it, life itself is the Sisyphean task of trying to please mothers, trying to meet their expectations. Men are said to "live for her and die for her" as they try to meet them. (2)

What is worse, from the male perspective, the mother never really articulates what she wants. She "urges her son to perform great feats for her, never really letting on what it is that will finally satisfy her. . . . She will never tell him and he will never find out." Nor are we just talking about infancy or early childhood in a man's life. This is a forever situation. The mother is said to remain forever at the center of her son's life. "You can't divorce your mother." (3)

Alex Portnoy, in Philip Roth's all too familiar rendition of the Jewish mother-son relationship, *Portnoy's Complaint,* feels he is being killed by his mother's expectations. "I am the son in the Jewish joke," he tells his psychiatrist. Who is Mommy's good little boy? Her little *bonditt,* of course. "He doesn't even have to open a book — 'A' in everything. Albert Einstein the Second." And nothing is ever enough to satisfy Sophie Portnoy.

> But what could it possibly be? Mother, it's me, the little boy who spends whole nights before school begins beautifully lettering in Old English script the names of his subjects on his colored course dividers, who patiently fastens reinforcements to a term's worth of three-ringed paper, lined and unlined both. . . . [L]et's face it, Ma, I am the smartest and neatest little boy in the history of my school! . . . So what is it I have done? Will someone with the answer to that question please stand up! (4)

On and on Alex goes. He cannot stop whining about it:

> Mother, I'm thirty-three! I am the Assistant Commissioner of Human Opportunity for the City of New York! . . . I graduated first from every class I've ever been in! . . . Oh, why go on? Why go on in my strangled high-pitched adolescent voice? (5)

Alex pleads with his psychiatrist to understand what he is up against. "My wang was all I really had that I could call my own." He tells the doctor that he can no longer stand to be frightened over nothing and implores him to "bless me with manhood! . . . Make me *whole!*" The reader is left in doubt as to whether poor Alex can ever be "cured," though the good doctor does publish a paper entitled "The Puzzled Penis," in which he describes "Portnoy's Complaint" as a "disorder in which strongly-felt ethical and altruistic impulses are perpetually warring with extreme sexual longings, often of a perverse nature," which can be traced to "the bonds obtaining in the mother-child relationship." (6)

Men say sons both want and fear their mothers. They say, "what a man is frightened of, more than anything else in the vast possibilities of living experience, is dependency, regression to a state in which he becomes an infant in the care of his mother." (7) And with the advent of the contemporary sexual revolution, the situation is getting worse. According to social historian, Christopher Lasch, "In view of the suffocating yet emotionally distant care they receive from narcissistic mothers, it is not surprising that so many people . . . describe their mothers as both seductive and aloof, devouring and indifferent." (8) This wanting and fearing is said to be at the heart of the war between the sexes because almost all women with whom the son later comes in contact are unconsciously the symbolic mother.

From sons' perspectives, high maternal expectations are not all bad, however. They are, in fact, part of the "good" mother's responsibility. One has only to think of Freud's mother from whom Freud says he derived his intellectual courage and confidence, his inner sustenance. "My golden Sigi" is what she always called him. She appears to have existed only for him and would let nothing get in the way of the flowering of her great expectations for him. For example, when the noise of his sisters practicing at the piano interfered with young Sigi's concentration on his studies, "the piano disappeared, and with it all opportunities for his sisters to become musicians." (9) As the myth has it, mothers exist for sons alone:

> I could never really take it in that there had been a time, even in *der heym,* when she had been simply a woman alone, with a life in which I had no part. *Alfred Kazin* (10)

> She would spend her middle years turning me into the man who would redeem her failed youth. I would make something of myself, and if I lacked the grit to do it, well, then, she would make me make something of myself. From now on, she would live for me and, in turn, I would become her future. *Russell Baker* (11)

Mothers' expectations become a matter of male survival. While most men are uncomfortable living with the expectations they assume their mothers have or should have for all times for them, they feel they cannot manage without them. They are terrified of being cut off from their mothers, rejected, unloved, off center stage. "To have the image shattered, the body frayed, to recognize for the first time and with intense force that the woman who held him, nurtured him, loved him, can also be cold, removed, critical, demanding — that she can reach almost demonic depth . . ." is considered the worst of fates. (12)

Perhaps what really bothers sons is the incongruity of life itself, life as it is. It is for all of us in a sense less painful to be dependent on the expectations of another, the mother; someone else to guide us and judge us, someone else to be good for. But if one is dependent upon another for self-justification one's self-development is restricted by that other person, absorbed by it. The subject inevitably comes to resent the dependency. He wants to be more than simply the reflex of his mother. It all becomes part of the unfathomable mythology of mothers and sons, part of the web of hypocrisy that hold *the mother* forever responsible.

CONVERSATION WITH A THERAPIST

Early in my research for this study I spoke with a therapist named Sarah. She had been trained in classical psychoanalytic theory and was a mother of sons herself. I wanted to know what Sarah's clients who were mothers of sons were telling her about their expectations for their sons. To be perfectly honest, I suppose I also was looking for a quickie Freudian interpretation of these expectations from Sarah.

The interview began haltingly. It was a good hour into it before Sarah and I both realized, simultaneously it seemed, that we were not hearing each other. She was not hearing what I was asking, and I was not hearing what she was responding. Although I had known she had been working for more than seven years in a mental health clinic in an impoverished upstate New York town, I hadn't given sufficient thought to the implications of the socioeconomic status of her clientele for her responses. That was part of the problem.

Instead of telling me about Oedipal complexities Sarah was describing working conditions in the "sew" factories where most of her clients were employed. She was telling me about lack of unions, lack of benefits, lack of job security and opportunities for advancement, and minimum hourly wages paid year in and year out. She was telling me about unemployed husbands and teenage children, chronic alcoholism, drug abuse, obesity, depression, and despair. She was telling me about the effects of white middle-class prejudice and apathy toward poor black, Hispanic, and white women. She was telling me about poverty in America.

"Oh, I get it," Sarah said with a wry smile when the light hit us both. "You were expecting me to share with you the Portnoy's complaint stuff you figured I'd be hearing from my clients!" She then explained that her training had been geared to the kinds of questions I was exploring, but that it had long ago become irrelevant for her.

"Listening to these women the 'on the couch' way with long periods of silence and occasional hard penetrating glances to encourage the flow of those deep dark Oedipal passions was meaningless. Worse than that it was interpreted as hostile and nongiving by the clients. I had to devise new approaches, reaching out on what might be called a more surface level. I just couldn't let those long silences go on and on."

She explained why she had to change her approach.

"If someone is really having trouble with basic human relationships because there isn't enough food on the table or because her husband is always drunk and her mind is preoccupied with reality problems like these, you just have to talk about these things. The goal is to make her a more confident, organized person so that she can survive and you have to talk about how to apply for assistance, or how to get a high school equivalency diploma, or how to shop efficiently. It's things like this that really matter — what I call 'ego-building,' where ego means simply being capable of coping."

When it came to mothers' expectations of their sons, Sarah said she just didn't see any intense problems with the process, other than an occasional mother who might express concern that out of frustration with her situation in life she was hitting her son too often, or screaming too much. The issue of maternal expectations, she speculated, was perhaps more meaningful for another class of people.

"The women I see are so busy struggling to survive that there is no emotional energy left for this Portnoy business. They are just too busy for it. Their whole lives cannot be wrapped up in their sons. I guess I would have to say that they just don't have great expectations for their sons. They have some expectations, of course. They expect or want them to pass in school, to be able to find a job and hold on to it, and to stay off drugs and away from the law. They expect their sons to behave in such a way that they won't cause them any more reality problems. They don't want another thing to hassle with."

Sarah was not dismayed that her clients appeared to have no great expectations for their sons. In fact, she observed, in some ways "it's a lot easier to raise your son if you are very, very busy. You don't put quite the same emotional burden on the child." She quickly added that she didn't mean to imply that her clients were ignoring emotional needs. She found that, on the contrary, most seemed to relate to their sons very well. The relationships were often reciprocal too, with sons, even as young as nine or ten, quite able to provide empathetic comforting support to their mothers.

From her observations she speculated that perhaps the major difference between middle-class and working-class mothers of sons was that in the case of the latter the mother was not the central person in the son's life and sons were not the central people in the mothers' lives. However, she was concerned that we not think she was romanticizing.

"There is no question that the kid from the middle-class family gets a much stronger sense of his own importance because his mother has great expectations of him. He, as a consequence, usually has more ambition, a wider focus on the world, too, with this built-in cheering squad. In school we see again and again that when the child from the deprived family is tested at five or six he does just as well as the kid from the middle-class family. Then at sixteen he drops out of school. Usually his parents had dropped out and he isn't expected to do what his parents never did."

I remember leaving Sarah's office angry with myself and with everyone I'd ever read on mothers of sons. How dare we universalize maternal expectations or anything else about mothers! It is strange how we can read all the books in print on class and race struggle and then, when it comes to mothering lump them all together into one composite picture. We totally forget the layers and layers of struggles that are part of most mothers' total situation.

REALITY PROBLEMS

Many of the women subsequently interviewed could speak only of the struggles, of what Sarah calls the reality problems. Insufficient household incomes, unsatisfactory marriages, drug and alcohol addicted children, nowhere to turn for support for themselves. They are tired, very tired. Theirs are accounts of coping. Theirs are one-day-at-a-time stories of efforts to help their sons survive in a world not known to Alex Portnoy.

Alice is a 57-year-old mother of nine children. She, with quite uncertain support from her recovering alcoholic factory-worker husband, has raised her sons and daughters in a fifth floor walk-up in the South Bronx. Several years ago she lost her oldest son Joey, at age 30, to heroin. She recalls his teenage years.

"When he hit the drug scene I would go with it, stay with it, wait for him. What else could I do? My husband would go to bed at eleven and then hit me in the morning with what happened. I resented that he dared be angry when he wasn't suffering. His way of coping was to throw them out. This caused terrible scenes between us because I would certainly have thrown him out before I closed my eyes to any of my children's problems. They don't stand a chance if you close the door or turn your back."

Alice recalls the time Joey dropped out of high school.

"Joey called me from Florida. Said he was going to quit school and work down there. The next day I flew down and got him enrolled in a high school down there. This sounds like it was an easy thing to do but it was a lot of trouble and a lot of anguish. When you have a house full of children, some of them still in diapers, and at the same time you have one son trying to cope with a heavy problem like drug addiction. . . . It was just a nightmare."

Mothers at times are too tired to deal with the day-to-day problems of their sons. Some just do not have the strength to hear about them. Joan, an Hispanic short-order cook in a diner, describes an encounter with the high school principal.

"We had a principal who called me on the telephone and told me to get down to the school because my sons wouldn't get on the school bus at the snap of a hat and he told me they were hoodlums. I don't go for this telephoning and I told him that if they do anything wrong I give my permission for him to pick up a ruler or use his fist — punch them one. But, I said, don't ever call me again because my husband is real sick and I am working so hard and I am tired and I don't want any more phone calls. Well, I know he didn't believe how sick my husband was and how bad things was around here and he kept on calling me and then my husband upped and died and this principal finally realized what I meant. I hope he's still thinking about it."

Other mothers have major problems of their own to overcome. Janet, a single lesbian, 24-year-old mother of a ten-year-old son, has just returned from an alcohol rehabilitation program. Her expectations for her son, Cal, are bleak at the moment.

"He lived with me during the worst years of my drinking and he thinks I am still a drunk and he just has all these crappy attitudes towards life and towards himself. At ten he is just so cynical and it is sad. I feel like he puts a lot of the blame on the way our life was going on my drinking. Some of it is true and some of it isn't. It feels like he's always testing me now and it drives me right up the wall."

Janet recalls her dreams for Cal when he was a baby. She herself had run away at the age of 13 from what she considered to be "a strict repressive fundamentalist" home in order to have him.

"When he was born his father and I had high plans for the kid. He was never going to go to public school. He was always going to go to some kind of alternative school. And he was going to be one of those peace-loving, gentle kids. He wasn't going to watch TV, he wasn't going to eat junk food. And wow! All that slowly went by the wayside because things changed. For one thing you can't have no money and send your kid to an alternative school. And my health food craze passed and everything else just fell apart."

Janet realizes that she cannot cope with her son right now. She has arranged for him to live with her parents and for welfare to provide counseling for him.

"I realize that my relationship with my son has blown away; it's gone you know. I am so sorry I did the things I did when I was drinking but I didn't have a choice because I was sick. But now I am really putting an effort into smiling once in a while and I hope Cal will be able to do that too."

Although there are many sad coping stories from mothers in or near poverty there are many inspiringly hopeful ones too. There are the dreams of mothers for their sons. For some it is for their sons to have a college education. For others it is for them to have satisfying careers; or to lead morally and physically healthy lives. For most, however, it is primarily to have the economic wherewithal to survive. My findings were similar to those of Sarah, the therapist, in that seldom are sons of the poor on center stage. The worries of these mothers are many and varied. The future is seen as problematic, both for themselves and for their sons.

MATTERS OF TEMPERAMENT

Since one's own experiences determine to a large extent one's expectations for the future we would expect to find middle- and upper-class women expecting their sons, irrespective of temperament or ability, to lead lives not unlike their own. Certainly the women participating in this study with college educations or those whose husbands had college educations expect their sons to go to college.

Mother of two sons, 16 and 13. Of course they will be college bound. They are not the kind who could do carpentry or anything else with their hands. They wouldn't know what to do.

Mother of two sons, 31 and 29. It is hard to be a Monday morning quarterback. I was brought up to believe that children would go beyond their parents. If I had a master's they would have a doctorate. Neither of them really did shine in school and somewhere along the line I let go of those expectations. Of course, the bottom line was that they would go to college.

Interestingly, however, there are very few "my son the doctor-to-be" stories. As with the woman quoted above, when I was growing up in suburban America of the 1950s it seemed our parents invariably expected that we, or rather our brothers and husbands-to-be, would surpass them professionally or materially. This is clearly no longer the case for the products of the baby boom in post-industrial societies. Many of the women with whom I spoke expressed doubts that their sons would come close to becoming as "successful" as their husbands. Some explained their watered-down expectations for their sons in terms of the overall economy, others to such societal problems as "loss of traditional values," increased divorce rates, bad schools, lack of law enforcement, the prevalence of drug and alcohol abuse, and their own inadequacies as mothers.

More frequently, however, the mothers I have spoken with attributed their lack of great expectations for their sons to matters of temperament or personality. The plain truth, Freud and Beauvoir to the contrary, is that as sons grow up middle- and upper- as well as working-class women do not invariably expect them to be leaders of men, destined for immortal fame.

This truth, I have come to conclude, is extremely painful for both mothers and sons. Why this is so is deeply mired in the murky mythology of the mother-son relationship itself; particularly the components of unconditional mother love and maternal transcendence through the lives of sons. Mothers of sons are conditioned to believe in the centrality of that relationship in their lives as sons are conditioned to believe they really are (or should be) that very center for their mothers.

This particular topic of expectations for sons is unhinging for many. To have less than great expectations seems somehow sinful, particularly when, as is usually the case in multiple son families, mothers have greater expectations for one son than for another. Mothers acknowledge their less-than-great expectations by focusing on certain behavioral or personality traits they find particularly bothersome or odious in various stages of their sons' development. But how, we need to ask ourselves, can it really be otherwise in human relationships over time?

Sally, a mother of two sons, eight and six, and a two-year-old daughter, talks about her relationship with Peter, the oldest; the differing expectations she holds for him and for his younger brother; and the guilt she feels for feeling the way she does.

"They are very different — one I relate to very well and the other, Peter, I have trouble relating to. I don't know for what reason that is. It could be because he's very much like me. When you see faults that are similar to your own you are less tolerant perhaps. My husband and I are always talking about how maybe I expect too much from him. He's the first child. I guess I worry that maybe he's too self-centered but then maybe all eight year olds are self-centered. I've always felt guilty about Peter which is of course very typical of mothers."

Sally explains how Peter was the only one of her children she didn't breast-feed and how she left him to go back to teaching because her husband was in graduate school.

"I agonized about that but I had to do it. And Peter was a premature baby and it was one and a half months before we got to hold him so I always felt that I never got that maternal bonding that Allen and Lisa had. I don't know. My husband says I shouldn't have these feelings and he's a super husband and a super father. I do think I've blown Peter's personality out of proportion."

She talks about her expectations. "It is just that you expect him to be a certain way — your firstborn. I expected him to be smart in school and he wasn't — he had to go to pre-first grade! To tell you the truth I really think it's good that he's gotten as far as he's gotten."

And his personality. "He's so reticient, no matter what you propose. He's not the type to say "Oh, Mom, that sounds like a good idea." Maybe I want him to be more enthusiastic, and more outgoing, more bubbly."

Her biggest challenge right now, she says, is to develop a good relationship with Peter because there are so many times when she gets upset with him.

"It's always I start blaming myself when I see this. You know, yesterday we were all sitting there talking and he was watching 'Little House on the Prairie' and he was explaining something to me and I looked at him and I thought how much I want to feel like I do when Allen and Lisa talk to me. I want to feel the same warmth. I feel bad. I know I place those expectations on him and I feel I fall down as a mother when he can't meet them."

We find, on the other hand, that for a variety of reasons some mothers just don't expect much from their sons. For Carra, a black freelance writer, it is a matter of interests. This is how she describes her 23-year-old son who lives at home.

"He is interested only in his stereo. He'll come to talk to me about his system for hours and he bores me. I hate to say it but he does. And I am a person who is interested in practically everything! But he tells me about stereos in such exhaustive detail that I go out of my mind. I feel bad about this because I recognize that he needs someone to listen to him. But I cannot do this. He bores me to death. He doesn't communicate at all — he monologues. That is the way he is."

Dot, a widowed factory worker, finds her youngest son, Tim, "just plain lazy," and now with her husband's "influence" gone, she says she expects he will always be that way.

"Tim is lazy — just that way by nature. He looks like his father, the blond side of the family, but laziness was never a trait in my husband! He was hyped up all the time, always going, always busy, like my oldest son. But Tim can just sit around all day. When I ask him what he's doing he says he's thinking."

Dot says she doesn't know anything about his "book work."

"He's in college now. Got himself some kind of a scholarship. There's no jobs around so I guess it don't matter. He tells me he gets good grades in school but I don't expect he'll know which way to turn when he gets out. I do know he would have known which way to turn if his father was still alive. I do know he'd have been contributing more around here too."

Lillian, an assistant professor of literature, finds her oldest son Paul, age 15, "depressingly serious."

"He is a different kind of boy. He's lacking a certain awareness of other people's feelings and he has no self-image. He just doesn't seem to have any light touch. Everything is drudgery for him. It's not that I don't have a lot of respect for him: he is a good boy in every respect. He is motivated to be a clean boy, a well-read boy, and you can appeal to him on his future. Every mother's dream I expect — but not mine."

Lillian also feels guilty that she has a different relationship with her younger son, John.

"It's just that Paul cannot laugh at himself and I find it very difficult to respond to him affectionately and playfully as I do his younger brother. This is not really nice. But I am responding to two different personalities. It is unfortunate but I expect that is the way it will always be. As much as I think it's a mistake to treat my sons differently I think it is dishonest and therefore a worse mistake to treat them in a way that is not natural."

She reflects on the experience of mothering and expectations for sons.

"This whole business of mothering is very humbling. I'm sure I would be very smug if I had the sort of children who were full in every way — the beautiful, popular, confident ones. I no longer have any great expectations. I don't think anything in the future will shock me. I think I've had to change all of my standards and swallow my pride and become humble. But I wonder about some of those smug mothers. I think a lot of people just cannot admit they are not on top of everything."

SEX ROLE EXPECTATIONS

"Doing oral history," as noted in the introduction, is being frequently caught off guard and surprised. The issue of maternal expectations for sons is a perfect example. Instead of hearing anticipated "my son the doctor-to-be" stories from at least older, middle-class women we found women of all classes, races, and ages were questioning traditional sex role expectations.

Not surprisingly, the women's movement appears to have had a profound impact on younger women's expectations for their sons. They expressed grave reservations about the traditional masculine ones. One feminist, pregnant for the first time, expresses her desire for a daughter for these reasons. (13)

"I just went through a period of panic, realizing that it might be a boy. I don't think it is because I hate males or anything. It's just that after little boys go to kindergarten they seem to get caught up in the social system. I hate what that does to little boys. I see them become rude, nasty, little tyrants."

She doubts she could be strong enough to "fight the system."

"I was raised to be very, very uncomfortable if any male is unhappy. I am so afraid I would be like all those mothers who give their sons this mindset that they can do no wrong and they can succeed at anything if they don't let anybody get in their way. I know so many strong women who are perfectly normal pragmatic people except when it comes to their sons whom they serve like little maids. I do the same to some extent with my husband. If I had another little penis running around the house it would be like double jeopardy."

Young mothers with both sons and daughters frequently have greater expectations for their daughters than their sons. (14) Lisa, the mother of a four-year-old son and a two-year-old daughter says:

"I feel I have to make my daughter more independent than my son. He is male and he is going to be forced into the work situation. But I really want her to get out there too. I don't want her to graduate from high school and get married and settle down and raise a family right away. I just don't want her to do that. I expect her to get out of this town so she can see what it's like on the outside. I really feel like I have to start right now to make her understand that she has to be more independent than her brother in order to really live."

Lisa is anxious to get a job herself so that she can be a role model for her children.

"Then the children will be able to see that I am not always going to be there, that they are going to have to have their own lives, and I am going to have my own life as their father has his now. We will all have something to say to each other when we sit down at the supper table. I think it is especially important for my son to understand that you don't have to stay home in the kitchen to be a woman."

Sometimes, however, Lisa worries about "emasculating" her son.

"I tell him he can't hit and then I see other little boys in his nursery school doing exactly the opposite and not getting punished for it and I wonder if I'm doing the right thing. Who knows? I don't want to make a sissy out of him and maybe someday he'll be in a situation where doing that is the only way he can survive. The only specific goal I have for him is not to be mean to anybody ever. I expect him to be a gentle, loving human being and whatever else he chooses to do is up to him."

For women in their late thirties, forties, and fifties, who experienced the impact of the women's movement in adulthood, the matter of sex role expectations for sons is especially intricate and disquieting. Almost all interviewed in these age categories, irrespective of class or race, who have both sons and daughters have very little to say about expectations (in the traditional sense) for sons and a great deal to say about expectations for daughters.

Mother of two sons, 19 and 17, and one daughter, 15. What I'd like for my sons would be a good relationship with whomever they choose to marry. My daughter — I'd really hope she pursues a career and really gets it nailed down before she gets married. We talk about it all the time. I guess I want for her what I wish I had had for myself. To be a happy fulfilled adult is the best thing you can give your children. I think you only owe your children so much.

Mother of one son, 20, and three daughters, 21, 19, and 17. I would like my daughters to be independent and have a career. They are definitely students and I am thrilled. I just know they won't do something dumb like run off and get married. My son, I don't know about him. I just want him to be responsible for his commitments.

Some mothers are truly in awe of their daughters' accomplishments.

Mother of two sons, 27 and 25, and one daughter, 23. Joanna is really so much better off than I am. She is a person in her own right. She has a strong sense of her own identity and she's perceptive in terms of her own limits, her own boundaries. I have great confidence in her. She has somehow arrived at a place where I think a female should be. I mean she isn't doing any of the things I did. She owns her own house and she'll never let herself be stuck in a subordinate role with anyone. God, is she lucky because I know she isn't going to make the kinds of mistakes I did. When I think of all the troubles her brothers have had I am just sort of stunned that she is so together, so strong.

Mothers may long for their daughters to be less tradition-bound than they themselves were; sometimes more so than their daughters want for themselves. One mother of four sons and one daughter is able to see the irony and humor in her changing gender expectations. She describes a recent conversation with her daughter who has just graduated from college.

"She said to me: 'Mom, I just want to tell you that I want to get married and I want to have children and I want to be a minister's wife.' And she said: 'I know I am supposed to go off and see the world but this is what I want to do.' Now I have always said, since they were three years old, 'go off and see the world, go off and see the world.' Always my kids were to go off and see the world. I never thought about it consciously but my daughter was right — I had been saying that all these years. When she said it back to me I just laughed and laughed.

"The thing is — I would never want to be a minister's wife. I would want to be the minister, or the professor, or whatever. I had married too young and had lived the kind of life my daughter wants to live. So for her to say 'and I want to be the minister's wife' and not the minister is. . . . I know she was establishing where she is. But where is she? But still, I like that she said that to me because she is kind of affirming her own life. I said to her, 'Well, what I really always said was for you to do what you loved. I really just want you to do what you really love to do. All I ask is that you really know what is out there. So you make choices knowing what is out there and having some experience. If you want to be a minister's wife, if you *really* want to be a minister's wife, that is wonderful. But know what other options are out there.' But I really mean that. It is truly what she loves to do that matters."

CHANGING EXPECTATIONS

Women's changing sense of self is often at the heart of the matter of maternal expectations. Abby, a lawyer and mother of two sons, describes the process she as a professional woman went through.

"I am that middle generation. I am very different from my mother — you know, her attitudes and all — and my mother-in-law. I still don't feel completely free. The guilt feeling. I am supposed to be living for and through my boys. Like a good Jewish mother. I never thought of myself first, consciously. When I had the boys even though I had my law degree I was still not conscious of myself as a professional woman. My mother would say, 'but you can't leave your sons.' In the neighborhood where we lived the mothers would openly criticize mothers who went back to work."

As Abby recalls them, the several years she spent as a homemaker with her sons were unhappy and frustrating. The precipitating factor that made her decide to return to her profession when the boys were still young was the following conversation in a park.

"A friend sat down on the park bench with me and said that my son had told her son there was no such thing as a woman doctor. I said, 'My God! My son said that!' Right then and there I said to myself, something is wrong. I decided to verbalize about this, to tell my children who I was, not to feel guilty."

Abby feels that her decision to take her profession and herself seriously has been good for both her and her sons.

"It's been a long slow process but I am feeling very good about them and about myself right now. When I think of the future I feel that there is only so much I can do. They will be on their own. I feel more and more that it is their lives and I am trying very hard not to interfere. My identity is not tied up with them. I don't think it would crush me if one of them were a failure. My whole identity is not wrapped up in them. I do not feel I am only their mother. It has taken me a long time to realize that I am my own person, that I am competent in my field, that people like what I am doing. I think a tremendous burden is lifted because I have my own identity."

Many mothers have come to appreciate the changing expectations they experience with sons. Summer, a divorced woman in her mid-forties has an exquisite sense of the reality and complexity of it all.

"I'm quite a different mother now. I keep thinking I'm getting better and better at it. Maybe I'm not, but I surely have a different sense of motherhood. In the beginning I wanted my boys to be poets, writers, musicians, bohemians. That is the only way I could picture them because these are the things I love. I made them take ballet lessons and forced them to read for one hour a day. I just expected them to love to do what I love to do."

She laughingly recalls the following incident reflecting the mood of her household when the boys were growing up.

"I remember one Saturday morning when my sons were between the ages of three and thirteen and we had three foster children living with us too. Before going off to play I insisted that each one find a room or quiet corner of the house to either read or practice on one of the many musical instruments we had for one hour. The previous evening I had read to them a speech Winston Churchill had delivered to the graduating class at Harrow. Pounding his fists on the podium, he had said, 'Never, never, never give up.' Now, on this particular Saturday morning the boys were being extraordinarily subversive, just full of beans. Some were reading their books held upside down, others were playing their songs backwards. No one was doing what I expected of him. I was becoming madder and madder, and the situation was getting out of hand. Finally, in utter frustration, I announced I was giving up and they could all go to pot. With that declaration I stamped into my study, a little room off the living room, slamming the door behind me. Moments later a little white piece of paper emerged from under the closed door. The note said, 'Never, never, never give up.'"

Summer says she never has given up, or, as she puts it, "to be more accurate, I have never given up on what I now see is the most important gift I could give my sons — respect for their freedom." She is comfortable with the knowledge that they will not be poets, philosophers, musicians; that they prefer parachuting, motorcycles, and computers.

As with many of the mothers with whom I spoke, the turning point, in a sense the giving up of the great expectations, came for Summer when she decided to make a change in her own life. For her, it was returning to school.

"Though I had always loved my motherhood and had wanted many children, I began to see that my relationship with them had been tight, nervous, controlling. When I went back to school myself and became so busy with my own studies I found that instead of my always being after them to study I relaxed. As I started living my own life, becoming more achievement-oriented for myself, my sons, little by little, became more self-motivated too. This process of awareness was extremely slow but now as I look back I see that as I became aware of my struggle to be free, to gain my sense of self, they too became freer. We are warm, affectionate, and relaxed with each other now. The boys have a good sense of themselves and I love myself as a mother with a career and I think they do too. What they do with their lives is okay with me and what I do with mine is fine with them."

Summer no longer has the great expectations we have come to assume all mothers hold. From her account, we can reasonably assume that the Sisyphean task of pleasing mothers will not be the fate of her sons. They will not be going through life asking "What does she want from me?"

It is true that we all need some people to have great expectations for us, to believe in us. But, as we have seen, it is foolish to assume all mothers of sons do. Some not only do not have great expectations, they have negative ones, or none at all. The tragedy of it all is not that some of us do not measure up with noble expectations for all sons for all times. The tragedy is that we alone should be expected to do so.

NOTES

1. Simone de Beauvoir, *The Second Sex* (New York: Random House, 1974), p. 576.
2. Philip Wylie, *Generation of Vipers* (New York: Farrar & Rinehart, 1942), p. 185.
3. Paul Olsen, *Sons and Mothers* (New York: Fawcett, 1981), p. 58.
4. Philip Roth, *Portnoy's Complaint* (New York: Bantam Books, 1970), pp. 39, 2, 14.
5. Ibid., pp. 123, 124.
6. Ibid., pp. 35, 40, frontpage.
7. Olsen, *Sons and Mothers*, p. 41.
8. Christopher Lasch, *The Culture of Narcissism* (New York: Warner Books, 1979) p. 301.
9. This incident, recounted by Anna Freud years later, is quoted in Betty Friedan, *The Feminine Mystique* (New York: Dell, 1974), p. 100.
10. Alfred Kazin, *A Walker in the City* (New York: Harcourt and Brace, 1951), p. 122.

11.   Russell Baker, *Growing Up* (New York: Congdon and Weed, 1982), as quoted in Carole Klein, *Mothers and Sons* (Boston: Houghton Mifflin, 1984), p. 77.

12.   Olsen, *Sons and Mothers*, p. 48.

13.   Approximately two-thirds of the women interviewed stated their sex preference at time of birth was for a son. Among the younger women sex preference at time of birth was evenly divided.

14.   My findings are contrary to those of Carole Klein, *Mothers and Sons*, who argues with the traditionalists that mothers are overwhelmingly more concerned with their sons' worldly success than that of their daughters'. Ironically, it is usually argued that black women have long been more concerned with the success of their daughters than of sons, thereby perpetuating a mother-centered family pattern. (Whitney Young, *To Be Equal* [New York: McGraw-Hill, 1964], p. 25; Thomas F. Pettigrew, *Profile of the Negro American* [New York: Van Nostrand, 1964], p. 16.)

5

COMMUNICATING

Men and women may speak different languages that they assume are the same, using similar words to encode disparate experiences of self and social relationships. Because these languages share an overlapping moral vocabulary, they contain a propensity for systematic mistranslation, creating misunderstandings which impede communication and limit the potential for cooperation and care in relationships.

Carol Gilligan (1)

IN A DIFFERENT VOICE

When I ask women in mid-life what they talk about with their children, those with both sons and daughters recall in detail their most recent conversations with daughters. There is generally ongoing dialogue between mothers and grown daughters, sharing of experiences and emotions, supporting of one another. This is not true for sons. The conversations they recall generally focus on their sons' worlds of school, work, or relationships on a markedly more superficial level. Mothers tread cautiously with sons. As Adrienne Rich points out, there is a "fear of 'alienating' a male child from 'his' culture" that still runs deep among women. (2)

The theme of this chapter is that the ways in which mothers communicate with their sons are reflections of some of the problems of communication patterns between the sexes. The patterns are conditioned by the historical subordination of women in the public sphere combined with their temporary dominance in their nurturing relationships with children at home. They are also conditioned by the current questioning by women and men of the contemporary gender system. it should come as no surprise to us that the communication patterns of mothers to sons are frequently characterized by such affectivities as peacemaking at any price, fear of confrontation, suppressed anger, and limitations on the sharing of experiences.

With the publication in 1975, of Carroll Smith-Rosenberg's "The Female World of Love and Ritual: Relations between Women in Nineteenth-Century America" feminist scholars began to realize that women talk with women, including daughters, in a "different voice." (3) This different voice, to use Carol Gilligan's terms as discussed in Chapter 1, is a reflection of the ways in which women and men are psychologically different because women define themselves and are defined by others in terms of their relationship with others. This different voice, I argue, emerges out of the mothers' mothering assignment itself.

On an experiential level, most mothers in this study (irrespective of feminist consciousness or lack thereof) tell us in a variety of ways that they do speak in a different voice from their husbands (or the fathers of their sons), one that is more caring or nurturing. They tell us they wish their husbands and sons would speak as they do — more caringly. They also tell us that (in accordance with Nancy Chodorow's theory) they speak in different voices with sons and daughters. Because part of their responsibility for the raising of sons as they understand it is to help sons identify with fathers they find they must use another voice with sons. Often viewing their communication role in the family as that of mediator or conciliator between sons and fathers or other authority figures, they speak the language of the conciliator.

Yet they also question, sometimes resist, the celebration of this mediator role. In subtle ways they tell us they see the limitations of their assignment — an identity that encourages all too often dysfunctional or superficial one-way relationships with sons. "What do we want for our sons?" Adrienne Rich asks. She speaks for many women when she writes:

> Women who have begun to challenge the values of patriarchy are haunted by this question. We want them to remain, in the deepest sense, sons of the mother, yet also to grow into themselves, to discover new ways of being men even as we are discovering new ways of being women. We could wish that there were more fathers — not one, but many — to whom they could also be

sons, fathers with the sensitivity and commitment to help them into a manhood in which they would not perceive women as the sole sources of nourishment and solace. (4)

FATHERS AND SONS

Although slightly more than half of the married mothers said they had "close" or "moderately close" relationships with their husbands, they had many complaints, most of which were centered on difficulties communicating. (5) Of their husbands they say: He's too unemotional; he is just not involved with us; he doesn't want to hear about problems; he seems to fear intimacy.

In the eyes of mothers these communication problems affect sons. The majority, irrespective of marital status, feel their sons do not have close relationships with their fathers. And the inability or unwillingness of fathers to relate to their sons is the primary cause. (6)

Mother of two sons (ages 20, 17) and daughter, 15. His father always found him [Billy, the oldest son] difficult to relate to because he didn't play ball or do the things his father did when he was a boy. That's all his father seems to think fathers should talk about with sons. I know it drives Billy crazy. He is always trying to make his father love him through his excellence — the carrot he will never attain.

Mother of a son, 22 and a daughter, 18. Mark [the husband] doesn't share much. He was always busy when Tim was growing up. He tried to be good with him but it was always such an obvious effort. He just doesn't feel comfortable discussing feelings. I know that is pretty average but I guess I expected more from him. I thought he was more culture-free than that. Tim is still very angry about this.

Mother of son, 21. I don't think my husband was ever comfortable talking with Peter as a person. It may be why he [Peter] is in this awkward state of affairs now [problem with drug abuse]. They never really built a relationship of trust.

Mother of son, 19 and a daughter, 16. My husband is a New England stoic. He believes in being in charge. That's the way he is at work but when he comes home he is tired and always on that raw emotional edge. In reality he's not in charge of anything but I can't say this to him.

To many mothers' dismay, as their sons become men they often see their sons becoming relationally like their fathers.

Mother of son 27, and three daughters ages, 19 to 33. The only thing my husband had feared was intimacy. He would do anything he could to run and keep running from it, keep very very busy. When Jimmy was about twelve I think he began to fear intimacy too. He began to follow his father. He knew he wasn't going to get strokes from his father by being a lovely, kissy, communicative boy!

Mother of a son, age 30. I find it ironic that after a lifetime of antagonism my son as a grown man is becoming more and more like his father. They are alike regarding sociability for one thing. I love parties and people and that was always a bone of contention between my husband and me. Now it is between my son and his wife. The same thing!

Mother of a son age 40, and a daughter, 42. I am seeing this stubborn streak in my son just like his father. Once he takes a stand on an issue he will not budge. It's like pride or something. There is no discussing the matter. Stubborn pride. That is exactly what his father has. They both act so dominant and strong. Sometimes I wonder if underneath it isn't because they are really insecure and don't want a woman to take over.

One mother finds her 21-year-old son even less communicative than his father!

"He's just like my husband was. My husband has now learned to communicate because I just bombarded him with verbal diarrhea for more than twenty years. Now he shouts back and stays because he knows I'll go on and on and on like a dripping tap until I've had my argument. But not my son. He is like iron."

Another mother describes how when her own father wants to get her dander up he says of her 22-year-old son from a former marriage, "He is just like his father."

"My father knows it drives me wild. When it comes to communication my ex-husband is a symbol for me of what I don't want my sons to be — lacking in ability to express connectedness, empathy, caring. My son knows his sisters and I feel this way and he likes to teasingly say to us: 'I am getting more and more like Dad.' In subtle ways I know and he knows he is not joking. In many ways he is becoming more and more like his dad."

This mother says that when her son was an adolescent rebelling against his father she would say over and over again: "Deep in his heart your father loves you — it is just that some men have trouble showing it. Be understanding. Be nice." Now she says she wishes she had added: "But don't be like him." Yet, she acknowledges, "both my son and I tacitly accept the cultural imperatives of 'becoming a man.'"

As mothers see it, this problem of communication men have is what troubles the relationship between fathers and sons. As primary caretakers, it is mothers' responsibility "to make it better" so that sons can learn to identify with fathers. The irony is that in order to accomplish this task mothers frequently feel they must encourage in their sons the very communication patterns they so dislike in the fathers. They do this by their very willingness to assume the role of peacemaker or mediator. A mother of four sons, ages 18 through 25, speaks for most of the women in the study when she says:

"I see myself as the mediator between my husband and our sons. I always pave the way if they've got something to discuss with their father. I am really the diplomat in this family. Everyone communicates through me. That is my primary role."

ON BEING THE PEACEMAKER

Given the ideological imperatives of the Reagan administration in this terrifyingly violent world where we are all victims of an international system of competing nation-states, it was with reluctance and trepidation that I first began to hear what women are saying about this role. Although the stereotypical image of the peaceable fairer sex, like all stereotypical images, is highly questionable (the record shows that women all over the world generally follow the leadership of their respective countries on issues of war versus peace), women on an interpersonal level are more inclined toward an ethics of peaceful resolution of conflict. (7)

Still, the questions they raise have to be heard. Many of the women express ambivalence and often downright anger with their identities as mediators or peacemakers between fathers and son.

"To be in the same room with them is to set my stomach churning. I am sick to death of it."

"I've lied for my son so many times just to keep the peace that I hardly know how to stop it."

"Boys take advantage of their mothers if they possibly can, without any scruple."

In subtle ways women are asking: when only the mother is peacemaker what price, for whom, and for what? For many of the women, peace itself is avoidance of conflict between fathers and sons, little more. The price, as we shall see, is often the mother-son relationship itself.

Betty, at 45 is beginning her own small business after years of part-time employment in a variety of areas combined with homemaking. She has two sons, 20 and 17, and a daughter, 15. Her husband is a highly paid executive of a large corporation. It is the quality of the relationship between her husband and her oldest son, Lee, and the role she plays in that relationship that concerns her.

When Lee was young doctors discovered he had "weak knees" and, according to Betty, this marked the start of the problem between Lee and his father because the condition disqualified Lee from sports.

"Jerry [husband] tried to understand the full implications of this physical disability but he couldn't. Jerry is the kind of person who is just super at whatever he does. He has never had any trouble with anything in his life and so he could never understand this kid who was always struggling to be like his father."

In Betty's eyes, Jerry's relationship with his second son is excellent, a situation she finds unfair.

"The middle child always did his own thing. He and his father are very close. But he is a natural athlete and a natural student. He doesn't need me. Do you know what I mean? This is hard on me when I see the two boys together with their father, the one cuddled up to him, the other outside, wanting very much to come in."

Lee is now in college pursuing a career in business administration, trying to follow in his father's footsteps again, as Betty sees it. She realizes it is time for her to get out of the picture in part because she is not needed in the same way.

"For one thing, I have no skills to offer this kid now. I used to be able to tutor him in French and English but now that he is in his father's field they can talk about that at least."

There are other reasons why Betty feels it is time to detach herself from Lee and his father. A part of Betty wants to abandon the mediator role for her own psychic health.

"You know, you get tired of being this intermediary. Being the sponge for everyone else's pain, being the only shoulder there is to cry on, being the only one for whom they can utterly fail. There have been days when I have been so obsessed with what was going on between Lee and his father that I hardly knew who *I* was or what *I* felt about anything. You know, you only owe your children so much."

Betty says she is determined to let father and son learn to communicate on their own terms; but not without a great deal of painful ambivalence about the future of the relationship and its effect upon her son.

"I think that when I get out of the picture it may be rocky for a while. But if I stop coming between them — this is my hope — they will be able to give each other some good strokes now that Lee is going into the same field.

"I really know that I must step out of the picture. I can't keep protecting Lee from what it is like in the real world. And hopefully Lee will have enough self-confidence so that if his father does. . . . You see, I am so afraid of the damaged psyche, of his father saying something that will really hurt him. I worry about the scars people carry around in their subconscious. I want to protect him, but by protecting him I am ruining that relationship with his father.

"I tell myself over and over again that I must allow Lee and his father to meet on their terms and to let what happens happen. But after all these years of being in the middle it is very, very hard for me."

Betty concludes that her son and his father need to learn to communicate without her for their sake as well as hers. If it does not work out for them she hopes there will be someone else to take her place in Lee's life.

"What I am learning is that I have to have my own thing and I must not be so involved in my children. It's not healthy and they are going away and I am stuck here thinking I gave my life to my kids and they aren't really caring about me. In my heart I know I was really doing it for me, sort of ego aggrandizement. Now I've got to figure out what I really

want for me. So what I hope for Lee is that he can find a good father —
and maybe I shouldn't limit it to his biological father — who will accept
him. It may be Christ, it may be his new dean at college, or it may be a
wife someday. I just know that it is so nice to have somebody on your
side, somebody you can relate to. But I have managed to survive without
a father I could communicate with and I suppose Lee can too."

Toni is 55, mother of three daughters and a son, age 27. Like Betty
and most of the women in this study she also emphasizes her role as
mediator in her family, particularly between father and son. However, as
Toni sees it, this is more or less the way it was in her suburban social
circle — fathers had the last word. She did what she felt she had to do.

"I was the counterbalance with all of my children. My role was to
always understand their position and I always did. I never agreed with
Tom [her ex-husband] intellectually or emotionally and I certainly never
agreed with the way he raised our children! I did respect him but I never
agreed with him. I always picture myself, those years when the children
were small, as sitting down at one end of the long dining room table, the
warm, artistic, liberal mother, with Tom at the other end, the
authoritarian, demanding, rigid father. (Not that we often sat at this table.
Tom was always away on business.)"

It was her son Tommy's position with his father she found most
disturbing. It was "always very competitive, tough, demanding."

"I remember, for example, the time when we gave Tommy tennis
lessons. One day Tom came home and said: 'Jesus! I saw you trying to
play tennis. All that money we are spending on you!' Tommy silently
turned his back to his father, went upstairs to his bedroom, and threw his
tennis racket out the window. That is how they communicated. It nearly
killed me to see him hurt Tommy so."

Toni recalls another incident when Tommy was about 13 or 14. It
was during the 1960s and Tommy wanted to wear his hair long. It was
very important to him. At breakfast one morning his father told her that
he wanted his son to get his hair cut before he returned from the office
that day. Toni recalls dutifully making an appointment with the barber for
after school. When Tommy came home from school she told him she had
made the appointment as per his father's request. She recalls that Tommy
turned around silently and went to his room and closed the door.

"I followed him and found him lying in the embryo position on his
bed. I will never forget this. It hurts me so to this day. I sat on the edge
of his bed and I said: 'Tommy, do it for me.' He got up and we went to
the barber. When we returned home he went upstairs to his room and

kicked the walls. I sat at the end of the dining room table by myself. I put my head in my arms and cried. When Tom came home I said: 'I never want you to put me in that position again. Never. It is your son and if you want him to do something he doesn't want to do you talk to him yourself.'"

Toni recalls saying that to her husband, but it didn't change the way the three of them communicated. Tom gave the orders, Toni disagreed with them, argued with her husband about them, and in the end tried to see that they got carried out so there would be peace between Tom and Tommy. "But," Toni concluded, "I always got beaten down. I never won my point."

Toni describes a difficult decision she felt she had to make when Tommy was 16. She and Tom had been divorced for several years and Tommy, after dropping out of the demanding prep school his father had attended, was living with her and attending the local high school. He was going through "a rebellious adolescence," as Toni puts it, and she finally called Tom and said, "I can't handle him."

"I knew that I was not in control. I knew I wasn't helping him. He needed the man, I felt, the father, to lead him into the jungle and teach him the ways of the world. I had done my job as Mommy."

For Toni, Betty, and many mothers the role of peacemaker between father and son is fraught with contradictions. Both Toni and Betty see a gentleness and openness they want to preserve in their sons. Both also see a toughness and aloofness in their sons' fathers they believe essential for their sons' welfare. Neither appear to be convinced the "points" won as mediator are worth it. Neither believe they have been successful in keeping the peace either.

CONFRONTATIONS

When women define peace in the family as merely the absence of conflict, as many do, their communication with sons becomes limited to the noncontroversial. They feel impelled to sweep their differences with sons under the carpet. They often find themselves in the position of avoiding confrontations at great cost to their own self-esteem, growth, and peace of mind, with little if any benefit to sons and husbands. As long as the mothering assignment includes the responsibility for making sure that fathers and sons get along, it is argued here, there can be little opportunity for real communication among mothers, sons, and husbands.

"I am afraid of confrontations," says Caroline, a mother of three sons, 33, 30, and 25, and wife to a man 17 years her senior. "When my boys displeased me I would try to work it off in my own head. I tried awfully hard to be controlled and mature. I don't suppose I pulled it off, but I tried. We never had any real confrontations. I just skirted around issues with them. I still do."

She recalls with amusement how the stage for nonconfrontation with her first son was set early.

"I remember one day I was bathing my infant second son and John the oldest was two and a half. He took off out the door and I had to run after him with this wet baby in my arms. When I caught up with him he was not apologetic at all, not a bit sorry. I told him to go in his room and think about what he had done and come out when he could say he was sorry. Two hours later after dead silence I went in to find him sound asleep. I had to wake him for lunch. He would never apologize. That is how all our confrontations have gone ever since. He always wins [laughter]. Although John is a person who always seems to be trying to understand the other's point of view, certainly with his political activities, he is always in complete control of me."

Nicole, a mother of two sons, ages 20 and 17, and a daughter 23, is more mercurial by nature than Caroline. She does, on rare occasions, have confrontations with her oldest son, Charles, but she feels painfully guilty about them. She describes Charles as "such an internal person."

"I have spoken to him consciously on at least two occasions on his need to learn to communicate — that for all human beings it is bad to bottle up as much as he does."

She finds him uncompromising. When she tries to get him to do something her way he refuses on principle.

"First, he will swear at me — which I actually don't mind a bit. At least he is saying something. Then if I persist and follow him around the house to make him answer me he'll go out of the house in the middle of the night. He's like a stone, Charles. Nothing can shift him. Certainly not me — I rant and rave and beat on him and I cannot budge him. Ever."

She finds his behavior and her own extremely distressing. "I absolutely hate him when he does that. But most of all when I confront him I hate myself." Irrespective of whether or not she feels she was right she always ends up apologizing to him.

"I hate myself for doing it with Charles because I know one I'm not going to win; and, two, it's doing bad things to him. And I do apologize afterwards, immediately. I'm apologizing for the lack of control. I'm not apologizing for the content of what I said."

As they see their sons become more like their fathers and as their own generally nonconfrontational communication patterns become rigid, Caroline and Nicole appear to tread increasingly cautiously, almost deferentially. Angry or frustrated as they may be with the communication habits of their husbands and sons, it is with almost reverence that they describe their sons as young men.

Of her three sons, Caroline says, "It is so interesting to me to have these sons so certain of themselves, of what they are. I would have used the word 'masculine' before the women's movement but we don't like that word anymore. Still, they have so much self-esteem. I do respect that."

And of Charles, Nicole says, "He has such intellectual stature, a really fine mind. It's of far better quality than mine. I think that's why he's so spare with words. He's got a marvelous sense of humor too. And I sometimes feel that he must feel what a leaden heavyweight I am. If only I could have a little more leavening of humor. I can laugh at jokes but I'm not a humorous, witty person. And I wish sometimes I were more subtle. But I'm thinking, I'm hoping to develop that side of me."

Of course there is nothing wrong with mothers having noble thoughts about their sons. However, when they are combined with suppressed anger and fear of confrontation the relationships become damaged. Within the framework of mothers' identities as peacemakers such deference may lead to situations where confrontations are in order and not forthcoming. In my conversations with mothers I discovered that many with post-adolescent sons unlike most with daughters have a long list of topics they feel they should place in an "off limits" category. These vary greatly but include sex, politics, and drug and alcohol use.

Listening between the lines, I sense that women are wondering whether they have been too solicitous of their sons' privacy, thereby closing doors that needed to be opened. For example, a mother poignantly describes how her fear of confrontation made it doubly difficult for both she and her son to come to terms with his homosexuality. Another describes how she could not bring herself to ask her son about his experiences in Vietnam, thereby shutting herself out of a part of her son's life both he and she needed to share.

It is confrontation of drug and alcohol abuse in sons, however, that most seems to frighten contemporary mothers. Even for mothers having no reason to suspect abuse in this area, it seems particularly difficult to confront.

"I did finally get up my courage. But it wasn't until some time after he had graduated from college. I finally just asked him point blank if he ever tried marijuana. He told me that he did once because his friends had nagged and nagged at him. I feel very fortunate."

Most of the mothers with post-adolescent sons say they assume their sons have probably tried drugs. It seems to be an issue about which they choose to remain fairly ignorant.

"I don't really know. They are probably pretty straight. Though maybe the two in college. . . . I wouldn't feel comfortable asking them."

"I am sure they all, you know, they have all been into drugs. They are probably recreational pot smokers. There is no problem — to my knowledge. And I would probably know if there was because it would affect his performance. No. There couldn't be. He was president of the youth group at the temple and that type of thing. A leader, always a leader."

"My boys have never been angels. I know they come home drunk on weekends like all the guys do. I just get mad if they wake me up."

For several mothers interviewed the issue is sensitive because they themselves are occasional illegal drug users. (8) Five mothers confided they had on occasion smoked with their college age sons so as not to appear hypocritical. None had found it particularly pleasurable however. Most had found it disquieting. On the positive side one mother with young sons (five and seven) says she feels confident her sons will be able to "deal with any kind of drug problem because they have been exposed to them every day." It is only what they may say in the neighborhood and in school that worries her.

"I think the thing that bothers me the most is imparting to them that this is illegal and that we would rather that they didn't run around and tell anybody in the neighborhood that this was going on. You know how they talk to teachers cause there is a very thin line between a teacher and a parent in their minds. And you just hope to God it isn't going to give you any problems."

Some mothers feel ambivalent about drug use. One mother of an 18-year-old high school senior says:

"I have such mixed feelings. On the one hand I want him to do some of the experimentation. I did some really dangerous things at that age. I don't want him to be the kind of kid who comes home, does his homework, sits in his room, is a goody-goody. I'd rather he smoked a little dope. But in moderation. I want him to stop at a certain point and I'm not quite sure he knows where that point is."

For most of the mothers in mid-life, however, the issue of alcohol and particularly drug use and abuse in sons is an area of parental concern where they feel powerless, anxious, ill-informed, and confused. (9) It is in this area of substance abuse that I as interviewer sometimes felt I was being given paradoxical information. (10) On the one hand, mothers would angrily describe sons whose behavior clearly indicates they are to some degree dysfunctional because of substance abuse. They would talk about abrupt changes in moods, sudden decline in attendance or performance at school or work, impaired relationships with family or friends, flare-ups of temper, borrowing and stealing of money, heightened secrecy, and association with new groups of friends who are known to use drugs. On the other hand, they would go to great lengths to minimize or deny the problem. They attribute their sons' suspicious behavior to peer pressure or growing up rites of passage.

One middle-class mother first describes in detail the indulgent life-style of her 21-year-old son who was not working, not attending college, "not doing anything." When asked if he uses drugs she responds:

"I don't believe he smokes a lot. I can't be sure when he is high. Only there are times when he seemed more relaxed and peaceful. But I think it's under control. We don't want him to feel hemmed in or watched upon by us in any way."

She then tells me of the following incident that had occurred a year earlier.

"There was a shocking thing that happened. I was so sad that he was so unhappy. He was up in the loft of the attic and the ladder was there and the thing was open so I climbed up the ladder and I said, 'What are you doing?' I poked my head up. And he was sitting there, with this gas container on his knees sniffing the butane. 'Oh my God! What are you doing?' I screamed. 'Why do you do it?' And he said, 'Oh, Mom. I'm so bored.' And he looked so vulnerable and so sad. I was just filled with . . . pity and . . . horror. The container is now no longer in the house because by chance another friend needed to borrow it. We've never spoken of it again."

When "the problem" comes to a head and must be dealt with, mothers find it an extremely difficult process. One mother of four sons ages 18 through 27 describes her reaction to her third son's suspension from school because of drug abuse. She first talks about her own guilt — her slowness in recognizing his allergies in childhood, her overprotectiveness with him, her poor judgment in sending him to an inappropriate school. She describes how she and her husband got him into a treatment center and then, she, like several other mothers I spoke with, states that she "handed the whole thing" over to her husband.

"My husband was forceful and excellent. He handled it beautifully. I couldn't deal with it because by this time I was menopausal and I was also in my first semester at the university. He was masterful, he was wonderful. We don't talk about it an awful lot. We make it very low key."

Counselors in the field of substance abuse find that because of mothers' great sense of responsibility coupled with deep emotional ties and the belief that they can "make things better," mothers of afflicted sons often deny the problem. They forgive, cover up, make excuses, try to believe that drinking and drug-related incidents are isolated events that won't happen again, and avoid communication on the subject. Inside they feel totally responsible, angry, hurt, fearful, and inadequate. They are, because of these characteristics, often the primary "enablers" according to researchers in the field of alcohol and drug addiction. (11)

Alcohol and drug rehabilitation counselors have found confrontation to be an effective therapeutic technique. The addicted family member is presented a picture of the reality of his behavior and destructive patterns from caring family members. But the therapy can only work when the caring family members are willing to face reality themselves, take a stand, say what they are feeling.

Although happily only a minority have to suffer the anguish of being the parent of a substance abuser, women who define themselves as the peacemakers in the family are often fearful of "rocking the boat" on any number of other issues. They go to great lengths to avoid controversy. Confrontation is risky. It means saying "I feel I am right and you are wrong." Some shudder at the thought because they have experienced hostile or violent reactions. They have known the sting of sarcasm, accusations, and stigmatizations and they do not want that for their sons.

There is more than one way to confront another human being however. As a psychiatrist writing on love points out, in addition to the "arrogance" way (most common among teachers and parents, especially fathers) there is the "humility" way. The latter requires painstaking self-scrutiny of one's wisdom and motives. It amounts to a genuine extension of oneself and constitutes, in fact, "a significant part of all successful and meaningful human relationships." Without such self-aware confrontation relationships are invariably "either unsuccessful or shallow." (12)

> To fail to confront when confrontation is required for the nurture of spiritual growth represents a failure ... as much as does thoughtless criticism or condemnation and other forms of active deprivation of caring. If they love their children parents must, sparingly and carefully perhaps but nonetheless actively, confront and criticize them from time to time, just as they must also allow their children to confront and criticize themselves in return. Similarly, loving spouses must repeatedly confront each other if the marriage relationship is to serve the function of promoting the spiritual growth of the partners.... The same holds true for friendship. (13)

SHARING

Close as the mother-son relationship is reputed to be, along with the communication limitations discussed above I find that mothers generally share little of their personal lives with their sons. With the tendency to avoid controversial issues such as sex, politics, and alcohol and drug use in their sons' lives, they also are reluctant to share their own experiences. It seems as though women's fear of "alienating" a male child from "his culture" precludes disclosure of women's selves.

For many women between the ages of 35 and 55 — the group we are focusing on here — the decisions to make major changes in their lives when children leave home are momentously exciting. Frequently these days women return to school or enter or reenter the marketplace and begin to see themselves in new ways. These decisions and the changes they affect do not seem to be shared with sons. Rightly or wrongly many women assume their personal experiences are of little interest to their sons.

"He does not want to know about any work problems of mine."

"They get very tuned out when I talk about my job."

"They really don't want to hear about my day. I am amazed. As a social worker I come home with really vivid, juicy tales of such strange lives like that of a young woman who had incest committed with her father since she was 12, and the strange things that have happened to her since and the situation that I was in with her. And I think anybody normal would be utterly fascinated. Perhaps it's too raw for them."

"I've never thought about asking them what they think of my being in school. I've just assumed they find it sort of embarrassing."

"I am so excited about the things I am studying, but I don't share it with my son. It seems like sort of an egotistical thing to do."

Even the "good times" women describe with sons appear to be few in number and invariably center on the sons' worlds, not the mothers'. One mother of a 28-year-old son who is a Ph.D. candidate studying abroad describes a special visit she had with him recently.

"It was a beautiful experience. He toured me around Paris and if you want a tour guide — you want a kid who knows about all of the history — he is it! We just had a beautiful time. I could just ask a question and out all this history would come. It was wonderful fun. We talked constantly. Not personal talk – just good conversation."

Another woman describes a special outing to see a play and the Picasso Exhibit in New York several years ago she shared with her 21-year-old son.

"We don't often do things together because he's very private and separate. But this summer there was a period where he and I were alone together. I said, 'I'd love you to see this play and I would also like to take you to the Picasso exhibition.'

"And he graciously consented to come with me. I felt honored that he'd done me the privilege [laughter] even though I was paying. But first he laid down all the rules. He asked to bring a friend of his and meet me at the museum. Then we were to have something to eat and go to the theater. Everything was on his terms. I wasn't to whisper or nudge or say 'Oh isn't that lovely,' or anything at all. And I wasn't to ask him what he thought of it the minute it was over. And all these rules I accepted, all these things I mustn't do. I did manage to restrain my talkative, noisy self. And we had a great time. But that's quite rare."

Women seem to feel that discussion with sons — even grown sons — of personal problems such as illness or divorce would be too burdensome for them to bear. They fear "leaning" on them and choose to keep these things to themselves or share them with daughters instead.

Two mothers talk about their inability to discuss with their sons their cancer operations. Karen, a mother of a 17-year-old son, and two daughters, 15 and 18, has never told her son she had cancer. Both daughters have known for some time.

"I've never told my son about my mastectomy. That was something I was going to do this summer and I didn't. I know it sounds very weird and it strikes me as being terribly weird. It's on my mind all the time. The children were too young when it happened so there was no way I could have told them then although my daughter claims she always knew. The fact that I had a disease that could lead to death just seemed too cruel for children their age. So then, when do you tell them? Do you just say, Oh by the way? Somehow I never did tell my son. It's something I have trouble dealing with I guess."

Like Karen, Marilyn, a nurse with three sons ranging in ages from 20 to 29, and a daughter, 25, recalls how she found it difficult to talk with anyone, but particularly her sons, about her illness.

"When I had my first of two cancer operations it blew my mind. I couldn't talk about it. I couldn't say a word to the boys. I think my husband talked to them but I'm not sure. Not long ago one of the teachers told me that when I had been in the hospital the first time my youngest son, in fifth grade then, was so sad. He just moped around in class. She finally asked him what was wrong and he didn't say anything. Then about five days later he said he wanted to talk to her. So she took him aside and he was half in tears and he told her his mom was in the hospital and he didn't know whether she was ever going to come home. So she talked to him. (Whether or not he was getting any support at home I really don't know.) Of course my husband was working long hours as always and running back and forth to the hospital and he never communicated that much with the kids anyway. I feel bad about it now. At the time I only was aware of how much it hit my daughter.

"I've since wondered whether some of my oldest son's problems didn't stem from that time. I remember it was right after Happy Rockefeller and Betty Ford came out and announced their cancers. My son and one of his buddies sat in the living room and made smart remarks about how they had only one headlight now. And right after that, within a week, I had mine too. We never talked about it."

A woman, with three sons all over the age of 25, still does not feel comfortable discussing their father's illness with them.

"I just don't talk about personal things with my sons. Just before my husband retired he had a nasty operation, you know, a cancer operation, that scared me but they got it all out. And right after that he had an eye operation which was very rough. But I don't feel it's right to burden the boys. I'm not — we're not really that close. I mean when people are starting their own lives."

Sex and divorce are also on the taboo list for many mothers. One mother of two grown sons and a daughter says:

"Of course there are lots of areas I wouldn't bring up with any of the children. Say I had a sex problem with my husband. I would never burden any of the children because it's distasteful, I think, to most children to consider their parents having a sex life."

She does add that her daughter seems comfortable making jokes about her parents' sex life and seems quite aware and happy about it.

Toni, who shares some of her thoughts on her son's relationship with his father in the preceding section, states categorically:

"Of course you don't talk to your children about marital problems. You just don't. Of course they hear Mommy crying and they see Daddy stomping out. And they hear bellowing in the bedroom or whatever it is that happens. But you must try to preserve a certain amount of dignity. You must."

Unfortunately, she acknowledges, the feelings are there and kids cannot help but pick them up. Her divorce was a bitter experience for Toni, her husband leaving her for a younger woman. She knows Tommy felt her pain but was caught in a terrible trap.

"It was very difficult for Tommy. He was about fourteen, going away to school for the first time. He probably knew we were going to get a divorce before I did because my ex-husband had his bride-to-be bound and tressed and waiting in the wings and he would do audacious things like take Tommy to a sports event and she would be there too. Tommy knew. He knew things I didn't know then. And he was caught between . . . he was right on the buzz saw. I mean, it tore the kid apart."

One Thanksgiving Day, a week before the divorce was to be finalized, Toni decided to try to talk with Tommy about the divorce.

"We had a big family Thanksgiving dinner. It was snowing. I said: 'Tommy, let's you and I go out for a walk.' We walked for one hour. I would say, 'How is school? How are you doing?' You know, general things. And finally I'd say, 'What do you feel about Daddy and Mommy?'

"He never said a word. He could not speak. He just walked with his head down. Finally I stopped in the middle of the sidewalk and shouted: 'Say something, damn it, Tommy, say something!' I was so scared for him. He couldn't say anything. There was nothing he could say. He was just trapped."

Another mother of a son, 19, and two daughters, 17 and 20, recalls that she never spoke forthrightly to the children about her divorce for several reasons. For one, she felt they were too young to understand. (They were five, seven, and eight at the time.) As they grew up there were other subtle reasons.

"All these years I have hardly ever spoken against him. Although he remarried within a few months I never talked about what had gone on before. I thought it was important, particularly for my son, and I couldn't divide the children up and tell one thing to him and the truth to the girls. It seemed so particularly difficult for me to talk to my son because it seemed important for him to have a relationship with his father and I felt that if I told him anything I would poison it. I really didn't want to."

Child support payments came into the picture too.

"I suppose I didn't trust my ex-husband. He had never been a reliable person. I really needed the money, the child support, and I thought he would be the kind of person who would drift away completely if the children weren't responsive to him. I wasn't sure about the money part. I did think he had enough of a guilty conscience about the kids and me. But I felt that if the kids were estranged from him that might be the end of it."

She also feels she had some responsibility for the divorce.

"I felt my responsibility was all in omission. I got very wrapped up in the children. Also, maybe some people are capable of stronger romantic love. I was so crazy about him when we were going together but after we were married for a while I didn't feel that way anymore. Maybe he sensed that. Maybe during that whole year of discussion of divorce if it had come out that I had wanted him very much. . . . I didn't want him to leave us. I felt he had a responsibility to the children. But I could never say, I'll just die if you left me because I just love you so much. Because I didn't."

In spite of her silence, several years ago her son began asking questions about the divorce and his father. She knows that he has been picking up on her emotions all along.

"He asked me point blank if John [her ex-husband] was seeing Lynn [his present wife] before we were divorced. He says he has known all along they were and it makes him really angry. His relationship with his father and his stepmother is really bad. He is very condemning of his father. It probably would have been easier on him had I been more straightforward from the beginning. I just don't know."

Many mothers seem to believe that built into their responsibility for sons assignment are some rigid rules about communication. To be a loving, caring mother of sons is 1) to teach sons to identify with their fathers; 2) to keep the peace between fathers and sons; 3) to be nonconfrontational with sons; and 4) to protect sons from "the truth" about painful issues such as divorce, marital problems, illness, and even boredom. Many mothers withhold their opinions, do not speak their minds, avoid expressions of feelings and emotions, suppress their anger. In the line of duty as they define it they opt for a limited honesty and openness — one that hides the self and precludes intimacy.

NOTES

1. Carol Gilligan, *In a Different Voice* (Cambridge, Mass.: Harvard University Press, 1982), p. 173.
2. Adrienne Rich, *Of Woman Born* (New York: W. W. Norton, 1976), p. 205.
3. Carroll Smith-Rosenberg, "The Female World of Love and Ritual: Relations Between Women in Nineteenth-Century America," *Signs* 1 (1975).
4. Rich, *Of Woman Born*, p. 211.
5. Jesse Bernard, *The Future of Marriage* (New York: Penquin Books, 1973) concludes that many women have a low internalized standard by which they measure marital happiness. They say: "My marriage isn't great but beats being alone" or "My marriage is no worse than most I know." Lillian Rubin states: "This is the dilemma of modern marriage — experienced at all class levels, but with particular acuteness among the working-class families I met. . . . They talk *at* each other, *past* each other, or *through* each other — rarely with or to each other. . . . They are products of a disjunction between thought and feeling, between emotionality and rationality that lies deep in Western culture." *Worlds of Pain* (New York: Basic Books, 1976), p. 116.
6. There were exceptions of course. Four women felt their husbands had closer, more nurturing relationships with their sons than they did. Several felt both they and their husbands had close relationships, and in families with multiple sons several said their husbands had warm, caring relationships with a particular son but not with another.
7. Josephine Rubin, "Women and Peace," *The Whole Earth Papers,* vol. 1, no. 6 (Spring 1978).
8. Seventeen of the women interviewed said they had smoked pot.
9. Research shows that use of illegal drugs begins in the teens, peaks in early adulthood, and is more prevalent among males. Males are more likely to use marijuana, stimulants like cocaine, hallucinogens, narcotics, and solvents (glue, etc.). Females are more likely to use uppers, downers, and tranquilizers prescribed by

physicians. Frances A. Boudreau, Roger S. Sennott, and Michele Wilson, eds., *Sex Roles and Social Patterns* (New York: Praeger, 1986), p. 301.

10.   Of the 73 women with sons in their teens or older, 46 said they believed their sons do or did experiment with drugs at one time.

11.   New Horizons Family Care Program, Binghamton, New York, untitled leaflet.

12.   M. Scott Peck, M.D., *The Road Less Traveled* (New York: Simon and Schuster, 1978), p. 153.

13.   Ibid.

6

SONS AND LOVERS

Une Belle Mere est une etoile; il faut l'admirer de loin.
Old French saying (1)

CHANGING POINTS OF VIEW

When I ask mothers of young sons how they think they will relate to their sons' future girlfriends they often respond with comments like: "It's hard to imagine right now but I suppose I'll be insanely jealous like all mothers of sons are"; or: "I'm sure I'll feel I am in direct competition with this female and she'll probably never measure up and I'll end up the typical hated mother-in-law."

Yet, when I ask mothers of sexually active sons how they in fact do respond to their sons' partners it is quite a different story. They tell me: "I really just love my son's girlfriend. She is everything I wish I had been when I was their age"; or: "She is the best thing that has ever happened to him. My biggest worry is that he won't treat her right and they will break up."

I am not hearing the sad, bitter stories we have come to expect from the mouths of unfulfilled, overwhelmingly loving and smothering, jealous mothers of sons. Not at all. Some women, like Katherine the hospital administrator (see Chapter 2), do find their sons' partners inappropriate or repugnant for a variety of reasons. However, the three conflictive relationships revealed by interviews for this book involved subtle class biases toward the objects of the interviewees' sons'

102

affections, biases they probably hold for others too. Even if we read between the lines very closely, the sources of hostility are not the smothering love of sons and resultant jealousy of sons' lovers that all mothers are assumed to have. In an overwhelming proportion, the women interviewed appear to welcome with open arms other women in the lives of their sons. They certainly do not perceive themselves as enemies of their sons' lovers. What is going on?

We think of the power of the Oedipus myth and the literature of the social sciences. We think about Gertrude Morrel as the symbol of the seductive, devouring mother, that murky Jocasta men fear, in D. H. Lawrence's *Sons and Lovers*. How could Miriam, her son Paul's first love, or any to follow, ever have competed against so formidable an opponent? (2) We think of Bessie, in Clifford Odets's 1935 play that provides the caricature of the Jewish mother for Jewish mother novels to follow:

Bessie: A girl like that he wants to marry. A skinny consumptive-looking . . . six months already she's not working — taking charity from an aunt. You should see her. In a year she's dead on his hands.

Ralph: You'd cut her throat if you could.

Bessie: That's right! Before she'd ruin a nice boy's life I would first go to prison. Miss Nobody should step in the picture and I'll stand by with my mouth shut.

Ralph: Miss Nobody! Who am I? Al Jolson?

Bessie: Fix your tie! (3)

The voices of the women we have listened to are modest and tentative, but they give us good grounds for questioning the judgments of so many novelists, psychoanalysts, and social scientists. Mothers speaking for themselves tell us, first of all, that they do not view their sons as substitute lovers. They tell us they want their sons to have lovers of their own. Here as elsewhere they have their own point of view.

The reasons given are straightforward. They tell us they want their sons to love women, to settle down, to assume a commitment to family. They bluntly tell us they want their sons to grow up, go away, and live happily ever after with someone else. They want them to take responsibility for their own lives — emotionally and economically. For most, a girlfriend/lover/wife for their sons stands as relief from their own burden of responsibility. Quite simply these mothers are turning to other women for help.

If we listen with an open mind to mothers themselves we can hear different kinds of mother-son love stories — rarely murky or sinister — in all their complexity, poignancy, and joy. These women have much to share with us about their perceptions of their responsibility for sexually active sons; their visions for new kinds of relationships for a new generation; their identities as women who value commitment in relationships; and, finally, their thoughts on daughters-in-law.

SHARING THE RESPONSIBILITY

Marion is a 48-year-old high school teacher. She was divorced when her three children (two daughters and a son) were young. She raised them alone, with, in her opinion, only financial assistance from her former husband. They are now "out of the house" and she is celebrating the "empty nest" with a live-in partner of her own. Like many women her age, she feels it is "time for me."

Her son Andy, age 21, is the middle child. She says that until recently she had worried about Andy's future. Since his infancy she saw him as more vulnerable than his sisters. She feels this might arise from his being a male in an otherwise all-female household, or because he reminds her of his father, or because he has a "certain kind of temperament."

"Basically he was an unexceptional child. His childhood, when I think about it, blurs into a general impression of sports (baseball mostly), toy cars, dirt, toy soldiers, baseball cards, and love of money like his father."

She recalls that his adolescence was "unremarkable" also.

"He maintained his interest in sports, had a number of boyfriends, and also a keen interest in making money. But he was never able to develop the sport skills so important to him and he is rather too sensitive compared to the average adolescent boy. Also he had no worthwhile interests — the kinds that would lead to a career."

Marion says she has always wanted him to have a girlfriend. She thinks he may have had one in high school but she is not certain because he never brought girls home and he and his crowd always traveled in groups. During his first year at college, her oldest daughter told her Andy did have "a real girlfriend"; she was thrilled.

"Don't tell anybody I said this — but I was very happy when I heard he had this girlfriend Donna. Before she came into the picture every time

I spoke to him we would go through this litany of How are your classes, and How is the food in the cafeteria, and How is this, and How is that? And then, invariably, I would ask: 'Are you going out much?' Or, 'are you seeing anyone?' I just would have to ask those questions even though before I would dial his number I would say to myself: Don't ask! And I would hate myself after I did ask. But I just had to ask."

Marion wonders why the questions were so important to her. She answers herself.

"I guess I wanted so badly for him to have a girlfriend first of all, because I think that it's wonderful; secondly because we all — well, who knows about all — but I *think* that we all want to know that our sons are heterosexual and we don't really know that. I mean the girlfriends he had in high school were never really serious. I didn't know anything about those relationships. I didn't know if there was any sex involved. He wouldn't discuss that. I didn't know anything about it. I just wanted this established so I could stop worrying — thinking about it [laughter]."

About her concern she says it is all "crazy, just plain crazy."

"I don't know why I was ever concerned. I had no reasons or indications that Andy wasn't heterosexual. And this has always been a liberal household where those kinds of things aren't supposed to matter. I don't know. But also I just wanted him to have a girlfriend because I knew it would make him happy. It would make anyone happy. I wanted somebody to like him. I know that is so important — especially when you are away from home."

Whatever the "crazy" reasons, Marion recalls being "really thrilled" when her daughter let slip that Andy's girlfriend was living in his room.

"I felt *so* good about it. I mean, I had none of those negative feelings we are supposed to have — no jealousy. Just the fact that he had someone. And my daughter said that he was very caring with her."

Andy is now engaged to a young woman of 20 named Paula. Marion is very pleased and she admits she becomes defensive when her family or friends say "but they are so young." She feels love and a desire for commitment can come at any age.

Marion describes her first meeting with Paula two years earlier when she and her partner, Sam, visited Andy at his college.

"She was already living with him in an apartment he shared with some other guys. When she came out to the living room after we had arrived I just was astonished when I saw her. I mean she is just so beautiful — but in this warm way. She's about five feet seven inches. She has very long, blonde straight hair and a tannish complexion with very brown eyes but her eyes are just so warm and so open and she looks at people so directly that I was taken with her. I felt that she glowed! It was very touching to think that someone so lovely loved my son.

"Well, after we talked for a while and they were making lunch I said that I wanted to see Andy's room. I knew which room it was so I walked down the hall by myself. When I walked into the room I burst into tears. Tears of happiness. There were fresh flowers all over. There were all these beautiful things put out. Weavings on the walls. Plants all over. Little pottery things. All the things I like — all the natural handmade things. The afghan I had crocheted Andy for his birthday was on the bed. A rag rug. It wasn't like a student pad with rock posters everywhere. .

"I just stood there and cried. I felt that if he is in this kind of atmosphere with a person who wants to live like this then this is really wonderful."

When Andy and Paula told her they planned to become engaged Marion was even more delighted.

"My initial reaction — I tell you this with perfect honesty — I was thrilled. I was really thrilled. First of all I knew her pretty well at that point and they had been living together for maybe six or eight months. I think she is one in a million. Andy is twenty-one. They feel totally committed. And if they are going to be together, then why not be married?"

Since Paula has come into Andy's life Marion has sensed dramatic changes in her son. For one thing, she had long worried about Andy's involvement with drugs. Now she says she does not.

"Not long after he met Paula, Andy told me they were at a Grateful Dead concert in California and they couldn't get into the actual concert so they were in an anteroom with loud speakers sitting on the floor with a large group of strangers all holding hands and with closed eyes and they were communing in that way and for whatever reason he had not smoked, he was not high, no drugs, and he said that something happened to him — that he reached a level that he does when he is stoned — this state of euphoric feeling and, well, something happened where he felt that and it was such an overwhelming experience — he felt a community with these people he was with — like totally connected and high on this human transcendence — that kind of thing. He decided right then and there that he no longer needed the drugs, that he could get there without it. And he stopped smoking that day and never smoked again. That is what he told me and I think that it is so largely because Paula is not interested in drugs and because he is happy with her."

She also feels that Andy's basic values have changed. "They seem to center on the best of the sixties hippieish thing — that we should all give, that we should all share, that we should all do for one another, and I think that is wonderful. I hate to think about everybody wondering just how much money they can make when they finish school."

In her view, their life-style is not too bohemian. "He likes to live very well. It's hard for me to separate what's got to do with Paula and what hasn't. I mean he has a very nice apartment and he has decent furniture. He likes to have — I mean he has nice things around him. As I said it is hard for me to tell which — how much is her and how much is him."

Marion feels that Andy is becoming more sensitive, loving, and communicative too.

"She [Paula] is very open about what she wants. For example, one day she said to him: 'It is very important that you came to pick me up at the airport,' and he said that he didn't know that because she hadn't asked him to. And she said that she really had wanted him to and it made her feel really good that he thought of doing that without her having asked him to. I mean, she is very expressive of these things. In a way she is teaching him to be giving. They are so warm with each other and always hugging and holding hands. Looking out for one another."

Before Paula entered the picture Marion was very concerned that Andy would never finish college: "Every year he was going to drop out of college. In fact, he wasn't even going to go to college and I talked him into it. But once he was with Paula he stopped any talk of not going — not completing college. That was a goal they had in common."

She also worried about his finding a job once he did complete college. She no longer does. Andy has recently chosen a major in education.

"He recently said to me, 'I have to think about supporting a family. I want to do something that will earn me a living and what do you think about education?' I told him I thought it was wonderful. That's what he's ready for."

Marion senses that her role as mother is changing and she is grateful to Paula.

"Paula represents to me real stability for him. I don't feel this total responsibility for him anymore. I feel the two of them together — I mean they are so supportive of one another — I feel they could face the world together. I mean, I can't help but be happy."

Interestingly, she feels that Andy has similar feelings of gratefulness for her partner, Sam.

"Andy seems to have the same attitude towards me that I have towards him. He used to behave terribly toward my boyfriends when he was young. But now he says he loves Sam and I believe he does. I think he feels about Sam the same way I feel about Paula. He feels that Sam really cares about me, that Sam is really loving, that Sam makes me happy, and also that he doesn't have to worry about me because I have a partner. Also he likes Sam's type. I mean he is that way too. Both are people who care more about others than about money and both are warm and open. I don't know how deep it goes. Maybe it is just because he knows that I am happy and he doesn't have to worry so much."

VISIONS OF NEW KINDS OF RELATIONSHIPS

Irrespective of their ages, race, and class backgrounds, or viewpoints regarding "women's liberation," all of the women with sexually mature sons interviewed ultimately came to accept the "sexual revolution." Probably mothers of sons, like most everyone else, have always been more inclined to accept premarital sex for their sons — but not for their daughters or future daughters-in-law. Certainly the publicly acknowledged living arrangements of their sons and sons' lovers were not part of most of the mothers' own experiences when young.

For some it was difficult to accept at first. One mother of 65 years recalls her feelings when informed of her oldest son's and future daughter's-in-law living arrangements before plans for marriage.

"I suspected something was going on. But I didn't want to ask. They came to me. They were honest with me that they were living together. I am a very religious person and it was something that was not done in my family. I didn't like it but I accepted it. I don't know what else I could have done. I said he was an adult and he could choose his own life-style. I thanked them both for telling me the truth."

When his younger brother announced a similar arrangement several years later this mother laughingly states she "didn't blink an eye."

Some mothers express ambivalence. They find themselves awkwardly uncertain about what to do at times. One mother in her mid-forties describes the period when her oldest son, Jim, had his first sexual relationship at 15.

"He slept with her at the house! It was very awkward, especially with his younger brothers and sisters around. I don't know. Maybe we just should have laid ground rules. I don't know. We didn't exactly deal with it. It is just that some mornings she'd still be here. I would pull Jim aside and say: 'I thought you said Joan had a ride home? I told you I would have been happy to drive her home.' He would say: 'Well, she thought she had a ride home and then she couldn't get a ride because her brother had forgotten and then it was so late and we didn't want to wake you' and blah blah blah. I must admit the younger kids didn't seem affected at all. They just took Joan right into the family and acted as though it was the most natural thing in the world for their brother to be having an overnight guest of the opposite sex."

Another woman, also in her mid-forties, describes her feelings of loss when her youngest son left home at 18 to live with a girlfriend the summer before he was to begin college.

"I have such mixed feelings. I almost wish I had told him not to go although I believe it is good for him to go. I want him to be on his own. But I'll miss him. I was really enjoying having him around this summer. This was to be his last one at home probably. I really just love talking with him.

"Now that he is gone I have this feeling of loss. I don't think it is because he left with his girlfriend. I see her as a sharp girl who can hold her own and won't play up to this macho side of him I don't like. I really think she is quite perfect for him. I just feel an emptiness right now. I am sure it will pass. I feel this sense of sadness but I also feel a sense of excitement. I am so happy that he enjoys women and they enjoy him. I love to think of them together learning about each other."

Unquestionably, the majority of women with sexually active sons feel comfortable with the freedom their sons' lovers have as compared with their own when growing up. Because of it they often have visions of loving relationships for their sons quite different from those in which they find, or did find, themselves.

Kathleen, a 50-year-old mother of four sons (one of whom is now married) was raised in a strict Roman Catholic home yet speaks for many mothers.

"I can't believe this is 'Kathleen the good girl' talking like this. Boy, have I come a long way. I don't have any problem with my sons' girls staying over. As long as they don't want me to entertain them. I feel it's a lot better than a parked car somewhere. And I really just feel that too many marriages were rushed into just to sleep together. Quite frankly, I have envied them at times. Thinking back to my dating years. . . . I don't think the family is going to be destroyed. I think there is a lot more honesty now, more openness with sex and everything else. This herpes and AIDS stuff — this just seems a terrible shame to me. But maybe it just is that I don't have morals anymore! [laughter] I don't know. I think each person has to live his or her own life as he or she sees fit. I can't sit in judgment on anybody else for sure. I think a kid who didn't live with his or her intended partner before marriage these days would be crazy. They've got to be better off than we were. I know I would never have married who I did and when I did if things had been the way they are now."

Obviously, women like Kathleen are talking about a great deal more than their views on the sexual revolution and their opinions of their sons' girlfriends. Underlying their visions for their sons' relationships with women are all the complexities of their personal lives. They are talking about their own disappointments in love and marriage. With varying levels of consciousness they are talking about their own oppression. And, most significantly, by identifying with their sons' lovers they are making a statement about their views on men that needs to be further explored by us.

THE MAKING OF COMMITTED LOVERS

Few of the mothers I interviewed seem to take pride in their sons' masculinity as traditionally defined. Judith Arcana, in her book *Every Mother's Son,* is correct when she argues that what mothers really want, but are too fearful to express, is for their sons to be more like themselves, more "female." (4) They mean more female in the relational sense that connotes a commitment to people and relationships. They do not mean the superficial "New Man" sense so aptly described by Barbara Ehrenreich, the man who eats sushi and cold pasta salad and wants to be considered "sensitive" above all else. (5)

In their expressions of affection and concern for their sons' lovers, I hear many women acknowledging the tension I feel with one of my sons, an aspiring writer. It manifests itself in subtle ways, almost always involving a girlfriend. The following description (taken from notes from my journal of a visit I had with him several years ago when he was 21) may help to illustrate what for many mothers, and sons too, is a disturbing paradox.

I was in New York City one weekend in April for a professional conference. I decided to forgo the first night's activities in order to have dinner with my son who was completing his last year of college in the city. We had not spent any time together for some months and I was feeling very happy to be with him. After shopping for a graduation suit for him we leisurely strolled in the twilight, deliberating about where to dine. Suddenly he stopped and announced that he had invited his latest girlfriend to meet me for dinner. Although a bit taken back that he had waited so long to tell me, I said I would be delighted to have her join us for dinner. I meant it too. I have always liked his girlfriends.

As it was after six by this time I suggested he call her at once and arrange a meeting place. He hemmed and hawed uncharacteristically. "Should we include her or should we dine alone?" he asked me. Apparently the young woman had been waiting all day for his phone call. "It is your choice and it really doesn't matter to me," I said. "I think it would be very pleasant to have dinner with you alone but on the other hand I also think it would be pleasant to meet Diana. Whatever you decide is fine with me." "But," I added, "surely you must call her and tell her something. You cannot leave her hanging like this."

"You are right, Mom," responded my son. "I feel like a worm. I know she has been waiting by the phone all day. She is anxious to meet you and has looked forward to dinner this evening for a long time. And I know we three would have a good time."

"Then, what is the problem?" I asked as I watched him fumble for a quarter and inch hesitantly toward the phone booth on Fifth Avenue.

"The problem," he explained, "is that as soon as I graduate next month I have to end this relationship. It is the same old thing again. She is too possessive. She wants too much from me. She wants a commitment I can't give her. My writing and graduate school must come first and I have told her this from the start. She says she understands but she doesn't. Everyday she wants me to call. Everyday she wants to know what I am doing. Everywhere we go she wants to hold hands, hold on. And now if I introduce her to my mother she will think that everything is fine between us. It will mean that there is a possibility of commitment. And it will be just that much harder for me to say good bye."

"Well," I said, trying to be understanding toward my beloved son, and flexible about the evening's plans, while recognizing a familiar feeling of empathy and compassion spreading over me for this girl I had not even met, "why not call her and tell her my schedule got very complicated and we are obligated to be with some other people?"

"I could do that," he said, "But I can't bear to hear her disappointed voice on the phone."

"Then for God's sake, invite her to meet us somewhere. It certainly sounds to me as though that is what you feel you ought to do," I said, failing to hide my growing exasperation.

"Yes, I guess that is what I must do," he concluded. "But," he added, "I must tell you there is something else that is bothering me. Part of the problem is that I know you are going to like her; I know you two will get along just fine. What I really dread is that 'oh dear,' look from you. Your eyes will be saying 'be nice, be committed.' You just don't understand that I don't want to have that kind of a relationship with anyone."

Well, my son was right on all counts. The three of us had a lovely dinner at a small French restaurant on the upper East Side and we got along famously. I found Diana to be warm, attractive, and remarkably courageous. This young woman from the Midwest was determined to make it in the tough field of journalism. I liked everything about her, especially a confident sense of self she had. She certainly did not strike me as the clinging vine type my son had portrayed earlier.

However, that she was unhappy about the course of their relationship was all too clear. The conversation over dinner centered on what it takes to be a writer, with my son arguing that it requires being alone with no commitments. At one point, when he went to the men's room, Diana and I talked in a nonspecific way about men's fears of commitment, and in a specific way, about his. I tried to maintain distance from Diana. I certainly didn't want to see my son married at 21. Certainly, too, I wanted him to be able to do all the things that talented young men are supposed to be able to do at that time in life. But I fear the warmth and compassion I felt for her came through anyway. When he returned to the table both Diana and I looked a bit sheepish. He knew why, smiling wryly.

When we parted outside the restaurant I knew and Diana, I suspect, knew we would never see each other again. I also felt that I had, in some weird way, let my son down. The next morning I even called from my hotel to apologize. To apologize for what? To apologize for liking his girlfriend, for taking them to an expensive restaurant? I am not sure I really knew then why I called to apologize but I suspect he knew. At any rate he graciously thanked me for calling and assured me that everything was okay, that I was the way I was, that there were some things I just couldn't understand.

I now think I called to apologize because I knew that I had been more able to empathize with her needs, those of a stranger, than his needs, those of my son.

IN PRAISE OF MOTHERS-IN-LAW

Despite the prevalence of mother-in-law jokes and the voluminous testimony of sons and particularly daughters-in-law to her awfulness, 28 of the mothers participating in this study who were also mothers-in-law seemed to have reasonably normal, pleasant relationships with their daughters-in-law. They, like the women with unmarried sons, generally say they like their sons' partners and feel they have good relationships with them. Some, in fact, feel they are closer to their daughters-in-law than they are to their sons.

"She is like a daughter to me. Through her I am just beginning to know him now. He is very quiet and she has helped to bring him out. She's a very outgoing person. He has learned to be more outgoing through her rather than through me because I am a quiet person too. My son's wife is a good letter writer so I hear from them once a week. If it wasn't for her I wouldn't ever hear anything."

One woman describes the anger and loss she felt when her son had an affair and then divorced his wife.

"I was so thoroughly disgusted and angry. I mean, I couldn't believe what was happening. I just liked her so much. I just loved being with her. We always got along. I remember when they had the baby. I went to the hospital too. I felt so close to her. She is a person who likes to please everyone. I am that way too. We are very much alike. Oh God! When I think about it I get mad all over again and this happened more than five years ago."

Some women identify with their daughters-in-law in ways they cannot with their sons. One mother, a widow, is able to discuss with empathy the alcoholism of her daughter-in-law. She feels that her son's job as a policeman has been very difficult for her daughter-in-law. Her own husband had been a policeman and she says she well knows the loneliness her daughter-in-law experiences.

"I was very disappointed when Tom [her son] decided to become a cop like his father. I hated that job. I hated it because I knew how tough it would be on his wife. I knew because it was tough on me. Joan [her daughter-in-law] started drinking while I just got migraine headaches all the time. I hate her drinking and what it's done to my son's family. I feel so sad for all of them. But I cannot hate her. My daughter-in-law is absolutely wonderful to me. She is so good to me. She calls me 'Babe.' She says, 'Babe, I love you more than I love my own mother.' It's just that she has this one failing. I think it must be a sickness. I do talk with her about it. And she knows I hide my liquor when she comes to visit. I bought a book for her to read but she wouldn't open it. I said I got it for you because I care about you or I'd say 'go hang yourself.'

"Tom is very quiet and keeps things to himself like his dad did. You just never know what he's thinking. Just like his dad was. It used to drive me crazy. I know it drives Joan crazy too. Same as it did me. If only she'd stop the drinking and deal with her problems some other way!"

As with the women whose sons were having premarital relationships, the few mothers-in-law who expressed negative feelings about daughters-in-law usually talked about either commonplace personality differences or matters reflecting class differences.

"The thing that bothers me about my daughter-in-law is that she is lacking in ambition. She is just very slow in everything she does. It drives me crazy because I am a real go-getter myself.

"I find I often have to bite my tongue because she comes from a family that doesn't do things the way we do them. For example, when they are visiting us it would not occur to her to say 'good morning' when she comes to the breakfast table."

"I just can't understand whey she can't do something about her weight. I have offered to pay for whatever weight reduction program she wants to try."

In the cases where the daughters-in-law are perceived by the mothers as very different from themselves, there appears to be a remarkable amount of tolerance, even appreciation, for the differences. One upper-class woman of 60 who describes herself as the "traditional homemaker, wife and mother," and is extremely critical of "women's liberation," describes her daughter-in-law in the following manner.

"Corkie is very liberated. She fights the traditional side of herself. She very much resents that part of her mother, and me too, and fights it. I think she feels it is terrible the way I 'spoil,' as she would put it, my husband. But it's *my* choice as an adult. She doesn't seem to understand that. . . .

"They have a very different sort of marriage. She and my son sort of share everything — I mean the cooking, the cleaning, everything. It isn't what I would choose but I do think it is a strong marriage. I think it's an automatic give and take. . . .

"Actually, Corkie reminds me of someone I wish I had been able to be: her self confidence; her lack of inhibition. The assuredness of that whole generation regarding the kind of life they want to lead. It's a maturity we didn't have. I suppose we were just brought up differently."

Again, we need to stop and ask ourselves what is going on. The experts tell us:

> In our culture, the range of attitudes toward the mother-in-law is wide. Many people, especially women (who may be mothers-in-law themselves some day), like their mothers-in-law. Nevertheless, the mother-in-law is overwhelmingly named on all surveys as the most difficult of all relatives. Extreme avoidance is not customary but an alternative technique, the mother-in-law joke, is very common. (6)

Our lives as family members can be divided into three stages: our family of orientation, our family of procreation; and our in-law family. Why is there so little serious research on this third stage? A casual check of the indexes of marriage and family textbooks indicates that when in-laws are dealt with at all it is usually under "Marriage Problems," and invariably from the perspective of the daughters- or sons-in-law, not the mothers-in-law.

Lillian Rubin, in her sensitive portrayal of the lives of working class couples, *Worlds of Pain,* finds that it is usually working-class women, rather than working-class men or middle- and upper-class women and men, who complain regularly and vociferously about mothers-in-law, especially in the beginning years of the marriage. She speculates that this may be due to the simple fact that "most working-class men lived with their families and contributed to the support of the household before they were married. Their departure from the family, therefore, probably is felt both as an emotional and an economic loss." (7) Studies by Landis and Landis, and Komarovsky support Reuben's findings that this is primarily a female problem, particularly in the early years of working-class women's marriages. (8) Although the focus of these studies is on the daughter-in-law, not the mother-in-law, their conclusions are that it is the emotional and economic departure of the son and consequent sense of loss that makes for nasty mothers-in-law.

The voices of our mothers suggest something else. They suggest that the maligned mother-in-law is but another reflection of the silent Jocasta, of the mother without a voice. She like all mothers is a convenient scapegoat for a myriad of family tensions. It is often more comfortable to blame our mothers-in-law as well as our mothers for our husband's, our own, and society's failings than to confront them directly.

NOTES

1. Old French saying, roughly translated, "A mother-in-law is like a star, best admired from afar."

2. D. H. Lawrence, *Sons and Lovers* (London: Duckworth, 1913).

3. Clifford Odets, "Awake and Sing!" in *Masters of Modern Drama*, ed. Haskell M. Block and Robert G. Shedd (New York: Random House, 1962), p. 656. Also note Philip Roth, *Portnoy's Complaint* (New York: Bantam Books, 1970); Dan Greenburg, *How to Be a Jewish Mother* (Los Angeles: Price, Stern, Sloan, 1964); Bruce Jay Friedman, *A Mother's Kisses* (New York: Simon and Schuster, 1964).

4. Judith Arcana, *Every Mother's Son* (Garden City, N.Y.: Doubleday, 1983).

5. Barbara Ehrenreich, "A Feminist's View of the New Man," New York *Times Magazine, May 20, 1984.*

6. John M. Schlien, "Mother-in-law: A Problem in Kinship Terminology," ETC. 19 (July 1962), pp. 161–71, as quoted in Gerald R. Leslie, *The Family in Social Context* (New York: Oxford University Press, 1973), p. 315.

7. Lillian Rubin, *Worlds of Pain* (New York: Basic Books, 1976), p. 88–90.

8. Judson T. Landis and Mary G. Landis, *Building a Successful Marriage* (New York: Prentice-Hall, 1953); and Mirra Komarovsky, *Blue-Collar Marriage* (New York: Random House, 1962), p. 259.

7

TURNING TO UNCLE SAM

> When the army promises to make a man out of a young boy,
> what do they mean by that? . . . The army will strip a young
> male of his individuality, his spontaneity, his fears and
> compassion for his kind, and make him a walking being that
> obeys orders without questioning. He must be taught to be tough
> and strong, to not show compassion, to not care for other human
> beings — some of them he must learn to define as "enemies"
> who deserve to be killed. He must not show tenderness or
> weakness because such traits are womanly. And so he is taught to
> kill the woman in him.
>
> *Birgit Brock-Utne* (1)

WORKING FOR THE ARMY

Those who are concerned about both feminist issues and U.S.
military buildup need to stop, look, and listen to some new friends of
Uncle Sam. Among them are many tired, frustrated, and overwhelmed
mothers of sons. These women encourage their sons to enlist in the
service because they view the military as the only available means of
shifting the awesome responsibility of their sons' welfare from
themselves alone. There are two additional interwoven themes to this
chapter: first, our recruiters are very much aware of such support; and
second, feminists are not because they have not yet taken sufficient time
to listen to mothers of sons.

As we have seen, the myth has it that "every mother entertains the
idea that her child will be a hero," and the hero is, of course, a son. "A

son will be a leader of men, a soldier . . . and his mother will share his immortal fame . . ." says Beauvoir. Woman as second sex, as other, as the inauthentic one, seeks to define herself in her son's deeds, and what better path than that of patriotism. (2)

Pinky, the mother of General Douglas MacArthur, as portrayed by William Manchester in his biography of the general, epitomized this type of woman. For her, "patriotism, like piety, was an absolute virtue in its own right. The cause itself was almost irrelevant; what counted was unflinching loyalty to it." At bedtime she would tell her young son, "you must grow up to be a great man," and she would add, "like your father," or "like Robert E. Lee." That Lee and his father had fought on opposite sides didn't matter at all; what mattered was that they had fought well for the best interests of their country as they saw it. Pinky made it clear that this patriotism she was instilling in her son was also for her. For example, when young MacArthur at West Point suffered from a cadet hazing incident so badly that he was asked to testify before a congressional committee, she sent him a poem that ends with:

Remember the world will be quick with its blame
If shadow or shame ever darken your name.
Like mother, like son, is saying so true
The world will judge largely of mother by you . . .
Be sure it will say, when its verdict you've won
She reaps as she sowed: "This man is her son!" (3)

For some, woman's attempt to find meaning in life through her son's deeds is a noble endeavor. That beloved liberal of the 1950s Adlai Stevenson told the Smith College graduating class of 1955 that "women, especially educated women, have a unique opportunity to influence us, man and boy," and he wished each graduate no better vocation than "to inspire in her home a vision of the meaning of life and freedom" for her men. (4)

For others, it is less than a noble endeavor. Philip Wylie, also writing several decades ago, went so far as to argue that our patriotic vulturelike "Moms" literally love their sons to death by making themselves "into a sort of madam who fills the coffers of her ego with the prestige that has accrued to the doings of others." (5) And more recently Paul Olsen in his popular account of sons and mothers argues that the son "develops into the man he is largely because he becomes the living embodiment of that which his mother wishes and fantasizes men to be — or not to be. There is nothing he can do about it, and, as a consequence such sons remain on a profound level little more than children in many aspects of their lives." (6)

However noble or ignoble, women's willingness to "*travailler pour l'armée*" (7) has been considered to be part of maternal responsibility and practice by many mothers of sons. This "working for the army" mode of thinking is described by Adrienne Rich in *Of Women Born*. Rich recalls: "The first thing I remember hearing about mothers and sons, at the age of about six, was the story of the 'brave Spartan mothers' who sent their sons forth to battle with the adjuration: *with your shield or on it,* meaning that the young man was to return victorious, or dead." Such valour has been assumed to be part of maternal satisfaction. (8)

Yet from my conversations with mothers of sons I have discovered that many mothers today who encourage their sons to join the service have no such dreams of satisfaction and self-fulfillment. These women, mostly working class but also middle and upper class, are not expecting their sons to be heroes. They have no grandiose objectives such as defense of the country, patriotic duty, honor to one's family name, or glory to the mother. Rather, they speak in terms of "reality problems," of day-to-day struggles to keep a family together and survive economically and psychologically. Their concerns are expressed in prosaic but harsh phrases such as "getting him off my back"; "needing some discipline I can't seem to give him"; "too many others to care for"; "no money for college"; "no jobs around here"; and "got my own life to lead too."

For those who have not yet begun to question the mother-son myth such feelings may seem almost blasphemous. In fact, (as mentioned in the Introduction), myself a feminist and antimilitarist mother of three sons, I was not even "hearing" at first what many of the women were telling me. I believed, with many feminists, that women could not be supporting the military buildup because it is women who will "create a world of peace, with equality instead of hierarchy, leadership instead of domination, self-mastery instead of mastery over others, cooperation instead of competition, skills and talents used to draw people together rather than to wedge them apart and with caring for other human beings, animals, and plants." (9) I still believe this but know now that it must be in cooperation with men in a very different society than the one we have known.

These women who encourage their sons to join the military are not the "inauthentic ones" seeking authenticity through the deeds of their sons as described by Beauvoir. Nor are they the super patriots Wylie so derisively wrote about. They are our mothers, or friends, or women like ourselves or our wives, women who have been lulled into viewing the military as a benevolent institution to take care of their sons in a society that cannot seem to offer anything else, not even a job, much less an affordable education, or a sense of community and camaraderie, and a sense of self.

The portraits of the four mothers that follow raise new questions about maternal responsibility. On a broader level they provoke old questions about the very structure of a society in which the preparation for war often appears to be the easy way to provide for the well-being of our young males — much easier than attempting to go through the painful process of reconstructing a political, social, and economic system for peace.

While these four women have very different perceptions about their relationships with their sons, there are many similarities in their life circumstances. Each of these women knew poverty in childhood, married a working-class man, and is presently concerned about having enough money. As a consequence, each expresses concern about the financial security of her son. In addition, each woman characterizes her husband as having been, in varying degrees, an emotionally absent (often physically absent as well) father when the sons were small. She, like most of the women in the study, regards herself as the primary parent. And, most significantly for the purpose of this study, each feels that when her son turned 18 her responsibility for his welfare should have been but was not terminated. These commonalities color for each the feeling that in the transition-to-manhood stage of her son's life there was no place else to turn but to the military.

ANITA

Anita, a woman of 47 with six children whose ages range from 16 to 28, feels that the military service for Carl, the third oldest, was the only alternative to "total insanity" for both her and her son. She considers Carl her "biggest problem" in life. Now 25, he is an alcoholic and she takes a share of the blame for that. It began with Carl's birth, she thinks. Carl's older sister by 14 months had had a rare blood disease in infancy and the prognosis had not been good. Although her doctor had warned against it, Anita says she "foolishly planned" Carl because she felt she must have a replacement in case the sick infant died.

"When Carl came along he had all kinds of problems from the start, mental, not physical, and I think it was because I was in no condition to turn around and get pregnant again. When he was little I was still so overwhelmed with the other who was always sick and he was into everything. I'd hit him and hit him and he was the type of kid who would say: 'If it makes you feel better you can go ahead and hit me some more.'"

She also blames her husband, Bob, for Carl's problems. Both she and her husband had known extreme rural poverty in childhood, but because of that experience she feels she wanted the children to have as much material and emotional support as the family could possibly afford to give. Through part-time work she has been able to subsidize the oldest son's college education. In contrast, Bob, whom Anita describes as a "very intelligent but totally noncommunicating recovering alcoholic," feels that he is a self-made man (a machinist who received his training in the army when he was 18) and that there is no reason his children cannot do the same for themselves. He refuses to contribute his money to their education. Nor, in Anita's opinion, does he contribute emotional support of any kind. Anita thinks that this fact is related to Carl's drinking problem. He could never get his father's approval on anything.

"He would work closely with his father and he wanted to be a machinist too. He was always trying to get his father to say to him, 'You are doing a good job.' But Bob will never say that to him. Never. Because that is the way he is. And it hurt Carl."

Because of her years spent with an alcoholic husband, Anita feels she has always had a particular soft spot for Carl in spite of the problems he has caused her. Before Bob stopped drinking their marriage was stormy with many violent scenes often witnessed by the children. Anita feels she has "a compulsion" to defend Carl against the outside world because it was he alone who defended her.

"When Bob was drinking Carl always looked after me. He would stand up to his father and he was the only one of the children who would. The others would go to their bedrooms, shut the doors, and pretend that everything was calm and collected. But Carl, even when he was only eight or ten, would stand there defiantly and say: 'Don't you ever hit my mother again.' Oh, we really had some times. You would not believe the things that went on."

Anita says that she does not think about that part of her life anymore. She realizes that her husband's father had hit his mother and that is the way he was brought up. Now that she is working outside the home and her husband has not been drinking for four years she says she finds it easier to forget. But she knows that Carl has not forgotten.

She also blames the school system for Carl's problems. It did not, in her opinion, provide the supportive environment he needed in order to gain self-confidence. She recalls one particular incident when Carl was in second grade.

"I had rheumatic fever. I got sick in December and I didn't get up until May. I had three toddlers at home and the four older ones were all in elementary school. Carl's second grade teacher kept writing me notes: Come to school at once and talk with me about Carl. And I would write back, telling her that the doctor didn't even know if I'd ever walk again. And she would write back: If you won't come to school we will have to set him aside because we cannot do anything with him and we can't spend any more time with him. And that is what they did. They held him back and just set him aside and by the time he was in third grade he was convinced that he was stupid. And from then on, no matter what you told him he still thought he was stupid."

It was in Carl's senior year in high school that Anita came to the conclusion that the military would be the best place for her son. Since he had been "having lots of problems" that year she had taken him to see a psychiatrist at the local mental health clinic. The doctor had told her there was nothing wrong with her son, and that, she says "did it."

"He'd be drunk and smashing up the furniture. I couldn't handle him when he'd go into these rages. My God, he is six feet one inches, a big man. I was beside myself. If the psychiatrist said nothing was wrong what else was I to do?"

In December of his senior year Anita recalls giving Carl the ultimatum. "I said, 'Carl, if you can't straighten yourself up you have one choice, the service, because I can't take anymore and there are other children in this house.'"

Carl did enlist in the army during the second term of his senior year. Anita says he could not have graduated with his class anyway because he had not successfully completed the minimum requirements for graduation. And for a while it looked like the right decision for him, she recalls. His rapid rise in the ranks and ultimate promotion to sergeant confirmed her belief that the military was where he belonged. Unfortunately he left the army soon after his promotion because, as Anita understands it:

"He got married and the marriage wasn't working because he was drinking too much and she wanted him out of the service so he got out to please her and the marriage went down the tubes anyway and now he's still drinking and trying to find himself."

Although the military did not make Carl's problems disappear, Anita maintains that his years spent in the service were his best, and hers. (10) She continues to worry about him, especially when he calls home in the middle of the night drunk and depressed. But it is different for her now.

"When Carl joined up he left home for good. He still lives far away and that's good. He's got to make it on his own. He's got to take responsibility for his own actions."

DORIE

Like Anita, Dorie sees the military as a positive institution in the life of her son, Frank, but not because her son is or ever was "a problem." Rather it was because he was "too good." Dorie feels that the military was the right decision for Frank after high school because he needed to separate from her, to stop trying to please her. He needed to "grow up and become a man." College was out of the question because her husband could not afford it. Also, "Frank liked money and nice things and did not want to begin his life saddled with loans."

Dorie is a 50-year-old woman who came to this country from England in 1952 with her mother and future husband, Ed. For several years after she married Dorie worked as a domestic. Since the birth of her daughter and son (they are now 26 and 22 respectively) she has been "an American housewife." Now that her children have left she sometimes thinks to herself: If only I had some kind of a real job now. However, she emphasizes, she only has these thoughts once in a while, particularly at those times when her husband, a mason, gets laid off. But then she catches herself and remembers that those years she spent with the children were "so precious," and she has no regrets.

"Being there for them, being there when they came home from school. That's all I ever really wanted to do."

And, because her husband has always worked long hours, often six or seven days a week, she feels that was her responsibility, her job. However, she believes that always being there for her son "made him spoiled."

"I guess I really did spoil him. My husband was always working and I was there to do everything for my son. I cooked whatever he liked. If he didn't want what we were eating I fixed something else for him. Sometimes my husband would be bothered that I did so much for him. Like I would put the hair dryer right where he would need it in the bathroom so he would be able to sleep an extra five minutes before school. And we could have our special little times together, just the two of us, before the school bus came. I really did spoil him."

Spoiled or not, Frank was a paragon in Dorie's eyes. He was obedient, warm, active socially and athletically at school, a good student (though a bit "lazy" when he reached 16), and a good worker who always held after-school jobs to pay for his own expenses such as a car. The only thing Dorie recalls worrying about was his refusal to sleep at friends' homes or accompany his grandmother on trips back to England to visit family. She believes it was because he did not want to be away from her and this she found disturbing.

When he first visited the local recruiting office in his junior year in high school Dorie was supportive, and happy. "I was glad he was thinking about going away because I knew he'd grow up then." In addition, although Dorie is uncomfortable discussing family financial matters, she says that Frank's first trip to the recruiting office coincided with the first time her husband was laid off from work. They, a family for whom credit cards, installment buying, or loans almost constitute immoral behavior, were very frightened at that time.

Frank has now completed his initial obligation and has recently signed up for another six years. Dorie says he is happy and financially secure and she is happy and proud.

"Frank works in an exciting field where there is 'danger pay.' He is never bored and he tells me the sights are beautiful. He has seen parts of the country he would never have seen. He's been to Yellowstone National Park twice, to Utah, Ohio, and New Mexico. He went to school for six months and earned some college points. He rents a nice ranchstyle house with two other guys and actually makes money on his housing allowance. He also has two motorcycles and a brand new pickup truck."

When Dorie sees Frank's friends from high school who have remained at home or who "jump from one menial job to another or have no job at all" she knows the military was the right decision. She is especially pleased because "Frank has become a man."

"When I talk to him on the phone it is more like talking to a friend or a real man — not my little boy any more. In maybe six months he had changed completely thanks to the service. The neighbors never believed Frank wouldn't come right back home. Now they see that he is the only one among his friends who has really grown up."

Dorie thinks Frank will serve his 20 years in the service so as to be eligible for all the retirement benefits. She says she doesn't worry about him at all. She does not worry about what kind of a wife he will choose because, as she puts it, "I know that even if he chooses one that can't handle money he'll take care of everything." She does not worry about the risks involved in his job either. Because she herself had grown up in wartime England where she had lost her father and many others close to her, her neighbors often ask why she does not worry about the possibility of another war. She laughs softly and responds:

"When everyone asks me why I don't worry I say: 'Because I don't.' I just think that there are risks in everything and every son should go for at least a year or maybe a year and half to get away from home, to get trained, and to really grow up. They have to grow up. They have to be independent. There are so many mothers who say 'Oh, no, I couldn't take my son being on his own like that.' But they ought to be on their own. How else can they become men?"

GENEVIEVE

In retrospect, Genevieve concludes that the military for her two sons was a mixed blessing — a negative experience for the older son Harry; and an extremely positive one for the younger son John. Like Dorie, she had encouraged Harry to join at 18 primarily because "he needed to grow up," and like Anita, she had encouraged John to join because he was "a problem."

Genevieve, in her late forties, says she feels content with her life now that the boys are grown up (Harry is now 26 and John is 23). She confides that she and her husband Henry, an electrician, are closer than they have ever been in 28 years of marriage. Her days are busy with local church activities, sewing, and volunteer work at the local hospital where she counsels men and women who have diabetes. She herself has the disease and she feels she has a great deal to share with these people.

When her children were young, just before she discovered she was diabetic, she had gone to secretarial school and had worked part time for a few years. However, her husband is "old fashioned," she says, and he wanted her to stay home with the children. Now that they have gone he still wants her to stay home and she agrees with him that she would "lose it all in income tax," so it really isn't worth her getting a job. Summing up her life so far, she says she would not do it any other way. Yet, she confesses, there are times when she feels sad, especially when she sees her husband romping with his grandchildren. "Do most women our age have the problem I did — the husband working long hours and refusing to be bothered and the children being left entirely to the mother," she asks? She wonders if Henry with his grandchildren is trying to make up for what he missed with his own. She sometimes wishes, and she suspects that he wishes too, that he could go back and do it all over again.

Genevieve has always been close to Harry, the firstborn. Yet when Harry graduated from high school she "strongly recommended" that he sign up with the navy. In a sense the navy had become a family tradition. Henry had been in the navy when he married her, and her brothers, and father-in-law had also served. But there were more important reasons why Genevieve wanted Harry to sign up.

"Harry had some growing up to do. He was sort of socially backward. He never started dating until his senior year in high school. He wasn't the type to be interested in college and I really don't know what he would have gotten into had he not gone. He just had to get away from home, get some training in something, and learn to accept responsibilities."

Although Harry eventually did get skilled training in the service and now, eight years later, has "grown up," holds "a responsible well-paying job," and has a wife and two children, Genevieve believes, with the wisdom of hindsight, she made a mistake by encouraging him to join up.

"Personally for him now I don't think he was service material. He shouldn't have ever been in it. I came to that decision after — I don't know whether it was the group he got into or the entire service at that time — but it was drugs. There were some very bad years for all of us. I hate to think about them. He grew up too fast really.

For John it was a different story. She had never been as close to John as she had been to Harry. John, she feels, was not a communicative child from the start. However, it was in high school that she recalls his "real problems" starting.

"He wouldn't talk to anyone. Rebellious. That is what he was. It got to the place where we didn't know what to do with him anymore. I thought about taking the psychology route. He wanted to do just what he wanted to do. I sometimes think I went a little too far fighting him on this."

She thinks she might have been too soft on him too. "He wanted a job after school. I thought maybe that would help him. Then he wanted to buy a car. Well, Harry had never been allowed to buy a car. But okay, I said, I'll let him have a car. Then, with that car he hardly ever came home. No matter what I did. . . . "

Slowly she says she came to conclude that it was marijuana that was making her son "so rebellious." He had dropped out of sports in school, was bringing home poor grades, and would sit stonily at the table. The only adults he would communicate with were a pair of professors who taught at the local university. Undoubtedly due to their influence, Genevieve feels, John announced one day in his senior year that he wanted to go to college to become a geologist. Neither Genevieve nor her husband were pleased. They felt the idea was totally impractical and her husband said he'd never find a job as a geologist. Although they told him they would try to help him financially as much as they could if he really wanted to go to college, they both agreed he should join the navy instead.

Genevieve remembers the day John came home and announced he had changed his mind and had signed up with the navy after all. She was very pleased with the whole experience.

"I thought for him it was the best thing going. And it definitely turned out to be the best thing. He got schooling and then he got aboard a sub which was marvelous to me because there is an entirely different class of people there. And no drugs. It is like a small family group. You are under water all those months and you have to depend on each other. The officers are so much different than those on board a ship — sitting down and eating and mixing with the men. There is real communication between the officers and the men. And all the guys are well trained. It was marvelous for John. Especially the feeling of camaraderie. I think that was the main thing for him."

One of the highlights of her life, Genevieve says, was a particular visit from John shortly after he had had his first sub tour. He told her he was so sorry for all the trouble he had caused her and he finally realized how much she had tried to do for him. Tears still roll down her face as she recalls that moment because, she explains, she knows she did everything she could and "somehow miraculously things worked out."

"It used to be he couldn't stand to be home; he had to be running wild. Now he would come home on leave and spend every night with me and his father talking and talking."

After a three-year tour of duty John reenlisted, receiving a $14,000 bonus and tuition for four years at a college of his choice. All he had to do to earn this, Genevieve explains, was to join ROTC [Reserve Officer Training Corps] and promise to serve in the navy for another five years after college. John is now in his second year at college, doing well, and Genevieve says their relationship has never been so close. She knows John has "finally grown up" and she is thankful to the navy for that.

KAREN

The explanation Karen offers for wanting her 20-year-old identical twin sons Larry and Mike to enlist in the military service when they were 18 focuses less on *their* need "to grow up" and more on *her* own need "to grow up." Karen is a 46-year-old receptionist for a large corporation and a wife of a permanently disabled man who is no longer employable. She is deeply angry about the years she has spent in what she calls "a bad marriage" with a "morbid, noncommunicating, emotionally crippled man." Several years ago she enrolled in an assertiveness training course that she feels changed her life by helping her "to see that after spending all those years serving husband and children" it is now time for her "to get to know herself."

Like Anita, Dorie, and Genevieve, Karen knew poverty in childhood. And when her own children were growing up there still never seemed to be enough money. The boys worked at odd jobs from the age of ten, contributing to the family coffers. When they graduated from high school Karen saw no alternative for them but the service. There was no money for college and she did not know how else they could gain training in a marketable skill. Without specific skills she felt they would be unable to find self-supporting jobs. And she wanted them out of the house.

In her fantasy life she recounts how she dreamt of leaving her husband the day the boys left home. But nothing worked out as she had hoped. Her husband's disease took a turn for the worse; he became too ill to care for himself. Compounding his dilemma, only one of the twins, Larry, made it through basic training. Mike was rejected because of a minor congenital problem. Karen says her husband's helplessness and Mike's rejection have taken a great deal out of her. You know, God, you must hate me, she sometimes thinks to herself. She considers she has no choice but to stay with her husband for the remaining months or years of his life. But with Mike it is a different matter.

After being released from the service Mike came home and "was just crazy," as Karen describes him.

"He could not handle being home alone without his twin, and also his feelings of being a failure. For almost two years I would come home from work to find him face down on his bed crying. He would find a job, but then quit after two or three hours."

Karen says in desperation she took him in turn to a hypnotist, a counselor at the community college, and the parish priest. No one was able to reach him, she concluded. Fortunately in the last few months he has "managed to pull himself together" and hold down a job. Now, Karen says, she *really* wants him out of the house.

"I want him out. I really want him out. I can't explain it. For me I want him out so bad and I know that must sound terrible to you and I've never talked to anyone about this feeling before. But he's so close to me. It's not good. Oh, how can I describe it? Other friends say I am so lucky to have a son who cares about me. But it is just that I am only now beginning to develop, so to speak. I raised my kids and kept the house together and now there are certain things, certain areas. I just need space for myself."

As she sees it, her son's protectiveness is partially her fault. "It's because I was so helpless when they were growing up because of the way their father was. They took over, they were the men in the family. I guess that is the way I wanted it then. But now here is Mike still trying to take care of me and it's got to stop."

Karen has told Mike how she feels but still he doesn't leave. She views it almost as a "game" they are playing with each other, a painful one for both of them.

"It's crazy. Mike is so possessive of me. Like one night recently I went out to see my girlfriend. As I was driving I looked back and saw this kid of mine following me in his car. I deliberately shook him. And the next day, sure enough, he said to me, 'Where did you go last night?' I said, 'Why do you follow me?' and then I left the room. I knew he was hurt but I had to do that. I don't want to be possessed by anyone anymore."

From Karen's perspective, the past two years would have been considerably smoother for her had Mike been able to remain in the service. In fact, she says, Mike's rejection from the military was the worst thing that could have happened to both of them.

"Larry is doing so well and Mike would have too. He's somehow got to make it on his own now and so do I. All I know is that I have to find some way to get him out of the house."

OTHER MOTHERS

Among the women I interviewed it is not only working-class women like Anita, Dorie, Genevieve, and Karen who are turning to the military as a means of shifting responsibility of their sons' welfare from themselves alone. Their stories are in a sense more poignant because they see no economic alternative. Yet, middle-class and upper-class women turn to the military too. For example, one recently remarried wife of a corporate executive whose youngest son had been to an elite prep school and then chose to drop out of college after one year, stated matter of factly that she had said to him: "You are going to learn some discipline and you are going to learn how to support yourself. I have my own life to lead now. The army will be the best place for you."

Another woman, after describing in great detail her son's expulsions from several boarding schools, car accidents in which he was at fault, and a variety of lesser adolescent crises, shared her enthusiasm over her son's recent decision to go to college the ROTC way: "I just know the discipline and routine will be something he will come to accept as being right for him. It's something I just couldn't seem to give him."

A doctor's wife with two sons ages 20 and 23, the youngest of whom is in the marines, argues for universal military training.

"I have always thought it would be much better for boys if they had to go into the military two years between high school and college. Then when they returned they would know what they did and did not want and they might be motivated to — well, you know — to do something in college. And they would understand the value of money and quite a few things they just do not understand at seventeen or eighteen. If some sort of law was proposed I would be for it. I really think our boys are not mature enough to go to college when they get out of high school."

A businesswoman with three sons between the ages of 18 and 22, all opposed to the military, is very concerned that her sons "stop partying" and "settle down." The military is where she feels they should be.

"I think this period of time that our society is in is very lax. The children won't listen to parents, won't obey rules. For me, military training is good for them. It makes them realize that you have to obey rules in life. You listen to the commands and you do what is told. After a two-year period these kids would be ready to know what they wanted to do. I think it would really help them mature along the right path. Now that's my way of thinking. My sons say they don't want to go into the service and get killed. I say to them: 'You never hesitate to go into the car, sometimes half in the bag, going at high speeds. You are challenged all the time with the death rate of the road and that doesn't seem to worry you.'"

The purpose, it should be clear, is not to castigate these mothers of sons who view the military as a benevolent training ground for young men. As a mother of three sons, two of draft age, there are times when I can well imagine what these women are feeling, how they can be lulled into forgetting the real purpose of the military — to prepare for war. We all can. The point is that each of these mothers for a variety of reasons feels there is no place else for her son to go. Given some of their circumstances, can we quarrel with them?

THE MILITARY'S PERSPECTIVE

Dwight D. Eisenhower, several decades ago, envisioned the military as this sort of magnanimous institution these mothers are searching for. In defense of universal military training he wrote:

> Although I certainly do not contend that UMT would be a cure for juvenile delinquency, I do think it could do much to stem the growing tide of irresponsible behavior and outright crime in the United States. To expose all our young men for a year to discipline and the correct attitudes of living inevitably would straighten out a lot of potential troublemakers. In this connection — although I am sure that in saying this I label myself as old-fashioned — I deplore the beatnik dress, the long unkempt hair, the dirty necks and fingernails now affected by a minority of our boys. If UMT accomplishes nothing more than to produce cleanliness and decent grooming, it might be worth the price tag — and I am not altogether jesting when I say this. To me a sloppy appearance has always indicated sloppy habits of mind. (11)

Much as the mothers with whom I spoke were not concerned with the condition of their sons' fingernails or the length of their hair, they were indeed concerned with discipline, and the discipline it takes to get a job these days, to develop the skills to survive on one's own.

The military as a benevolent institution to guide our boys through the transition to manhood and economic independence is what one of the most popular films among college students several years ago, *An Officer and a Gentleman,* was all about. When Mayo, the officer candidate at the Naval Aviation School, breaks down before the sergeant and says: "I got nowhere else to go, I got nothing else," many young men identified with him and so did their mothers. The message of the film is that the military will get it all together for our young men (and, though with considerably less certainty, our young women too). And what mother does not want that for her son? (Mayo's mother had given up, swallowing a bottle of lethal pills when her son was 15.)

In the late 1960s many of us in the United States naively believed that after the lessons of Vietnam the military would never again be viewed as a humane institution. We argued for a volunteer army over a draft on the grounds that individuals' freedoms would be better protected and the military would become less powerful. We were confident then that alternative institutions like the Peace Corps or Vista (Volunteers in Service to America) would take its place. How wrong we were. After approximately a decade of fears of ending up "all black," or at least "all underemployed," the military appears to have succeeded beyond even its own wildest dreams. "Army Recruiting is Thriving as the Nation's Economy Falters," read a first page headline in the New York *Times* by the early 1980s. "We've gone double in terms of quality," and "numbers are up too," reported a recruitment sergeant. (12) In these times of economic hardship for many, the military has been so successful in changing its image (by raising pay, improving working conditions, and being more creative and energetic with recruitment) that many citizens, not just mothers of sons, have forgotten its very function.

There is scarcely a mention of the business of conducting war in the current recruitment literature. (13) This is what a current U.S. Army pamphlet tells our sons:

The Army is an education in more ways than one. At the end of your enlistment you'll have gained a lot more than money and college credits. You'll have experience. Responsibility. Maturity. And have a clearer idea of what you want. More specifically, if you join the Army you will:
1. earn over $500 a month to start [with room, board, medical expenses, etc. paid for],
2. continue your education now,
3. save up to $8,100 for college,
4. get valuable skills training [e.g., electronic technician, surveyor, plant equipment operator, carpenter, plumber, electrician, lithographer, drafter, machinist, automobile body repairer, radio communications technician, photographer, radio TV production coordinator, etc.],
5. see more of the world [e.g., West Germany, Holland, Belgium, Italy, Great Britain, Turkey, Greece, etc.].

A marine recruitment pamphlet entitled "Facts Parents Should Know About the United States Marine Corps" tells us that boot camp is where "the building of body, mind and spirit" of sons will begin. The pamphlet claims our son will be in top physical shape when he leaves; will receive good meals (5,000–5,500 calories per day of tasty, body-building foods), will wear custom-made uniforms for summer and winter made from the finest materials with a clothing allowance for replacements, and will enjoy excellent free medical and dental care. He will be encouraged to attend religious services and on off-duty time he will partake of a well-rounded educational and recreational program to ensure the mental and physical well-being of all. He will have the opportunity to make friends with people just like himself from all over the country, and these friendships will last all his life because he and his peers will be bound together by a common spirit of loyalty.

According to this same pamphlet, the relationship between our son and his officers will be

> in no sense that of superior and inferior, nor that of master and servant, but rather of teacher and scholar. In fact, it should partake of the nature of the relation between father and son, to the extent that the officers, especially Commanding Officers, are responsible for the physical, mental, and moral welfare as well as the discipline and military training, of the young men under their command.

Our son will be counseled to continue his education and there are

> numerous opportunities for special education and training in occupational specialties and through the Naval Enlisted Scientific Educational Program (NESP) which provides full pay and allowances, as well as tuition, to Marines who are selected to attend college on a fulltime basis leading to attainment of the baccalaureate degree.

If we wonder who will be watching over our son, the corps tells us that

> from the moment of his arrival at the recruitment depot to the day he is discharged, your son will be under the supervision of a Commanding Officer. This officer is charged with the responsibility of, and is vitally concerned with, the welfare of your son. On the welfare of the individual rests the welfare of his unit.

And this pamphlet closes with quotations from grateful parents:

Dear Sir, . . . We attended our son's graduation and couldn't have been prouder of our new son. . . .

Dear Sir, . . . I sent you a good boy who has very great potential and lacked only self-discipline — which is probably normal for him and his age. When I saw him at Parris Island he showed me that you have put him well on the way to maturity. . . .

Dear Sir, . . . I would like for you to inform the officers and enlisted NCO's . . . for the most efficient manner in which these men display competence. They can never know otherwise the transformation I had the pleasure to see in my own son. . . .

We cannot castigate the mothers who turn to the military in search for these things for their sons — education, maturity, self-discipline, training and skills, a job. We cannot even blame them for closing their ears to the stories of other mothers whose sons are dead or maimed. The fact is that the responsibility of mothering sons is overwhelming for many women who do not have the resources, financial or emotional, to execute successfully that assignment.

Whether our strong military institutions are supported by a draft, universal training, or volunteerism is no longer the central issue. For both mothers and sons, especially the poor but often the well-off too, the military is often all there is. For the poor after high school, jobs are few and the chances for an affordable education slight. For both the well-off and the poor the recruiting team is there, with its promise of discipline, training skills, camaraderie, and full manhood. The military grows and prospers while most of us no longer question why civilian life offers so many so little. The point is there has to be somewhere else for mothers to turn, someplace else for sons to go.

NOTES

1.   Birgit Brock-Utne, *Educating for Peace: A Feminist Perspective* (New York: Pergamon Press, 1985), p. 32.

2.   Simone de Beauvoir, *The Second Sex* (New York: Random House, 1974), p. 55, 576.

3.   William Manchester, *American Caesar: Douglas MacArthur, 1880–1964* (New York: Dell, 1978), pp. 56, 65.

4.   Adlai Stevenson, "Commencement Address," reprinted in *Woman's Home Companion* (September 1955), and quoted in Betty Friedan, *The Feminine Mystique* (New York: Dell, 1974), pp. 53–55.

5.   Philip Wylie, *Generation of Vipers* (New York: Farrar and Rinehart, 1942), p. 193.

6. Paul Olsen, *Sons and Mothers* (New York: Fawcett Crest, 1981), pp. 29, 88.

7. This literally means "to work for the army," and figuratively means "to accept the uses to which others put one's children," as defined by Sara Ruddick, "Maternal Thinking," in *Rethinking the Family,* ed. Barrie Thorne and Marilyn Yalom (New York: Longman, 1982), p. 84.

8. Adrienne Rich, *Of Woman Born* (New York: W. W. Norton, 1976), p. 192.

9. Brock-Utne, *Educating for Peace,* p. 143.

10. Anita either did not know or did not care to discuss the details of her son's departure from the military. From the interview it is not clear whether it was his or the army's decision.

11. Dwight D. Eisenhower, "This Country Needs Universal Military Training," *Readers Digest* 89 (September 1966), pp. 49–55.

12. New York *Times,* October 13, 1982, p. 1.

13. The recruitment literature (printed by the U.S. Government Printing Office) from which the quotations to follow are taken was collected from recruitment stations in the fall of 1982.

8

JOCASTAS UNBOUND

At twenty, most of us have painfully learned that stereotypes are a way of lying. By thirty, we discover the other side of the coin: that the stereotype is a way of saying a half-truth, of expressing the sprawl of reality, the contradictions of experience. To be sure, people and things are frozen, plucked out of time and history in the process, but there is always a wisdom at the center of the distortion.

Michael Harrington (1)

UNIQUENESSES AND COMMONALITIES

After the stories of Karen, Genevieve, Dorie, Anita, Toni, Betty, Marion, Summer, Katherine, and so many others how can we understand mothers of sons? What is there left to say? What hope is there for the relationship? For mothers? For sons? And who, if not mothers, are going to be responsible for the men of tomorrow?

Initially their stories, much as we may yearn to believe to the contrary, steer us toward the conclusion that these women are unique. Reading between the lines we cannot but conclude there are rich, poor, strong, weak, conservative, liberal, ambitious, lazy, proud, humble, open, repressed, untroubled, and troubled mothers of sons. There can be no such thing, contrary to the popular portrayal of them, as *the* mother of sons, or for that matter *the* mother or *the* woman. To deny them their differences is to deny them their humanity. We are reminded of William James's oft quoted passage:

> The first thing the intellect does with an object is to class it along with
> something else. But any object that is infinitely important to us and awakens
> our devotion feels to us also as if it must be *sui generis* and unique. Probably
> a crab would be filled with a sense of personal outrage if it could hear us class
> it without ado or apology as a crustacean, and thus dispose of it. "I am no
> such thing," it would say; "I am myself, myself alone." (2)

Unlike James's crab, mothers of sons can hear themselves being classified, pigeonholed for all times and places. Like the crab they want to cry out, "I'm no such thing, I am myself, myself alone." There are, of course, black mothers and white, Jewish and Christian, rich and poor, gay (three lesbian mothers were interviewed for this study) and heterosexual. To deny mothers of sons — and all mothers, all women — their differences is to deny them their humanity. The dire consequences of the stereotyping of them by society as reflected in the work of the social scientists and to some extent feminists themselves is in fact the focus of these mothers' perspectives.

But is there a wisdom at the center of the distortion? Is there some truth to the stereotypical portrayal of *the* mother of sons? Surely there are themes running through these stories that intuitively strike us as "typically female"; others as "typically mother"; and others as "typically mother of son." With the interviews for this study I have found these themes override ethnic, religious, class, or sexual preference differences. To ignore or be unable to hear the commonalities would be to deny the validity of women's history and experience. We want to tie the threads of this array of particulars. We search for the connections in these perceptions of women's relationships with sons.

Foremost, we are impelled toward some generalizations very much in line with social scientists' conventional stereotyping of the "good" mother and with recent feminist theory. (3) We know from reading between the lines if not from their very words that these women consider themselves the primary parent for their sons, the one *responsible* for their well-being. This responsibility, from their perspective, does not end when their sons reach maturity: it lasts a lifetime. These women generally define themselves as more nurturing and more emotionally connected to their sons than are their husbands. Because the major component of their mothering responsibility as they see it is relational they assume the roles of peacemakers or conciliators in the family, particularly with fathers and sons. These women do indeed believe they speak "in a different voice" from men, a more caring one.

Yet just as clearly we are impelled toward some very different generalizations about mothers of sons, ones that are disquieting for both women and men. These are the characteristics of what some would call the "bad" mother. Reflecting the institutionalized sexism of women's daily lives the leitmotiv of their perspectives on the mother–son relationship appears to be generally one of ambivalence about their nurturing-of-sons identity. We are led to question the long accepted notion that sons as "sexual others" who represent "power and status" play a unique psychological and social role in lives of mothers. From these perceptions we conclude that it is not at all clear, as most men seem to assume, that sons occupy center stage in the lives of mothers. In fact, we sense that mothers with both sons and daughters might be giving daughters center stage now. They certainly (again in line with Chodorow's thesis) appear to treat sons and daughters differentially, communicating more openly with daughters and frequently daughters-in-law. Nor can we continue to accept the old belief that mothers seek fulfillment in their own lives through the deeds of their sons. Further research on the mother-daughter relationship ironically might turn Beauvoir's thesis upside down. Mothers in the late 1980s are in danger of seeking an impossible transcendence through daughters rather than sons. In any event, the best most mothers expect from their sons is that they be self sufficient — economically and psychologically.

Underlying these maternal perceptions is the fact that women are questioning, irrespective of age, class, and the other variables of race, religion, and sexual orientation suggested, the responsibility for primary mothering of sons itself. They are not at all sure what "successful" raising of sons means these days. The "gender question" looms large. Its presence is reflected in these women's struggles for a sense of personal worth outside their identity as mothers and in their ambivalence (for lesbian mothers interviewed too) toward the masculine values they feel impelled to foster in their sons. Strongly emergent from these voices speaking out is the muddled, often breathless cry for something more in their lives than the responsibility for mothering sons.

Although we may find some truth in both the "good" and "bad" mother stereotypes it is certainly hoped that this "rhetorical" study "sees the wisdom in the distortion" but confirms neither. The book's most ambitious aim is to encourage a humanistic (empathetic) understanding of mothers of sons struggling in common with other women and men to balance the conflicting values of a culture that has for too long placed men and women in separate unequal spheres. It is to argue for a balanced view of mothers of sons; one that recognizes both the uniqueness and commonalities of them as of all human beings. It is to place mothers of sons within the context of their outer environment — what existentialists call the *umwelt*.

At this moment in history this means a call for a weaving of experience and theory by listening to mothers of sons. They, with all their particularities, are searching in common for the delicate balance between selfhood and caring for others. Women are trying to live in fuller ways than ever before. They are seeking unboundedness from "the idolatry of duty" (as feminist writer Ann Oakley defines the family) implicit in the myth of good mothering. (4) As both men and women come to appreciate the joyous excitement as well as the painful conflicts of women's efforts to balance their new and old commitments, the mother-son relationship will no longer be mired in the myth of the perfect mother who is every son's due. Rather the relationship will have the potential to be a true one where both mother and son share and care with a fuller knowledge of the human frailties and vulnerabilities of each other.

THE UNBOUNDING PROCESS

Although there are probably an infinite number of alternative routes, the three primary paths along which the women in this study are seeking that delicate balance between selfhood and caring are by 1) establishing close female friendships; 2) returning to school; and 3) entering or re-entering the marketplace. The first path, that of establishing female friendships, may come as a surprise to many, considering that the contemporary women's movement has been around for several decades now. To my mind this study confirms most feminists' contentions about women: "All women are feminists at heart. In their psychology lies a great love for women as a class. But it's interred beneath a mound of rubbish." (5)

A 35-year-old woman, a college student with two sons and a daughter all elementary school age, describes how she is just beginning to respect women.

"I love what is happening to me. I had trouble when I was younger. I never had women friends, girlfriends. I was never close to women. In fact, I'd say from the time I was eighteen until I was twenty-seven I did not have a single woman friend. My best friends were men. They were my husband [married at 19], my brothers, my brothers-in-law, and a few other men I knew. When we'd go to parties the women would be here and the men would be there and I'd be right with the men. I enjoyed their conversation more. The women seemed so boring. Suddenly my perception has totally changed. I can honestly say that now, with the sometimes exception of my husband, I like women better than men. I'm not afraid to say and think a lot of things now. It's like they give me permission to be me."

She says she observes the interaction of her children through different lens now too. When her daughter was very young she encouraged her to play with her brothers and their friends. Now she feels her daughter needs to play with little girls so it won't take her daughter as long as it took her to appreciate the female sex. Rather than encouraging her daughter to play with the boys she finds herself encouraging the boys to play with girls.

A woman with three sons, ages 12 through 18, who is employed as an office secretary and also attends college part time describes how her self-concept has changed because of female friendships.

"It took me a very long time to trust women and to be able to turn for support to women and to be able to share with women. I just felt that I could handle the boys and the marriage and go back to school and have my career and nothing would be compromised. Now I feel that I could never have survived without my friends. One of the best things that ever happened to me was to fall into a women's conscious-raising group several years ago. My God, we talked about things I would never have shared with a living soul! It was then that I came to realize that it was my responsibility to draw lines around where I will and will not cross, what I wish and do not wish to do. Now I can look my family in the eye and say I don't really much care to cook on a particular evening or I am sometimes really tired and damn it, I am working and contributing and it shouldn't all be falling on me. I'm feeling the boys and my husband have an obligation to the family too. When I come home from work I am not the maid. They hear that remark all the time and they groan but you know, they are beginning to do their share and we are all respecting, liking, and enjoying each other so much more."

Over half the women in this study have taken at least one educational course since marriage, reflecting the nationwide opening of educational opportunities for adults — often referred to as the "graying of the campus." After spending many years as a domestic, a 42-year-old single black mother of a 17-year-old son is now, with the help of social services, attending college. She feels her dreams are coming true.

"When I told my friends I was going to go to school they said 'you've got to be crazy.' How could I tell them I didn't want anybody telling me I was stupid ever again? Now all of a sudden I can just say: 'I don't care who you are. You will not down talk to me.' I'm such a completely different person than I was when my son was little. I just learned to keep saying: 'I'm gonna do it. I'm gonna do it.' So many beautiful things are happening. I'll be graduating from college and my son will be graduating from high school and starting college. It's really unbelievable if you consider where I come from. Growing up for me — well, only a little do I care to remember and ninety percent I choose to forget. If you've seen "Roots" [a television series based on the family history of black writer Alex Haley] you've seen my life. It is basically about not really having an identity, not really feeling good about yourself ever. That's not true anymore. The most important thing is that nobody including my son ever disrespects me now."

A mother of four sons describes what it has meant for her to return to graduate school. She chooses to focus much of her graduate education including her master's thesis on her search for the delicate balance for herself and her sons.

"I had problems. I don't know — maybe early mid-life. The meaning of life — that is what I was searching for. Then a lot of things began to come together in graduate school. It was just the tip of the iceberg really. I started learning how to learn on my own. The first hurdle was to learn to feel secure about the decision to go back to school because I could have had a real guilt trip. There were comments made in town. 'Where is your mother?' the boys were always being asked. That type of thing.

"Since going back to school I have realized that in our society there is so little opportunity for us to make decisions, to express our opinions, to become responsible for ourselves. Everything is told to us. In our family I now am trying to teach the boys that they have to be accountable to themselves. They have to be responsible ultimately for what they do. My master's thesis is going to be a framework for self-knowledge to show we are responsible for ourselves."

The majority of women interviewed work outside the home either full time or part time. Of the women who are "housewives," the majority plan to be employed in the near future. (6) While many of the employed women indicate they are conscious of and angry about the inequities of women's occupational segregation (the kinds of jobs they are able to get and the low wages they receive as compared with men), none say they wish they could stay home. A mother with five sons and a recovering alcoholic husband has recently become a sales representative for a company that sells housewares in private homes. She explains what her job means to her.

"I think the boys and my husband would have driven me over the bay, into the loony bin if I hadn't gone to work. We certainly needed the money but I really went to work more or less as an escape. I had to do something. I was at the point here where I was ready to just pack my bags and go. I knew I had to do something on my own. And I really have. I recently gave a speech at a rally. I was talking about setting goals — you know, you set yourself a goal and you plan on how you are going to get to the top, get to where you want to be. I still can hardly believe it was me talking. God, I feel great right now."

The money she earns has become important now too.

"If I want something I know I can have it. It seems crazy but it's like my place in the family has changed because of my paycheck. My husband pays the taxes, gas, electricity, phone and I am free to make decisions about the rest. For example, I am paying for Jim [the third son] to go to college. My husband won't pay for school for any of them. He says if a kid wants to go he can work for it. He says he's self-made and they can be too. He didn't need college and he doesn't think they do either. But that's not the way it is as I see it. Now I wouldn't fork over my money to all of them but Jim is so smart and reliable and he told me that when he gets out he's going to pay it all back. He will. He says he's keeping track of every cent. I feel so good about being able to make my own decisions about things like this."

The unbounding process along these paths is sometimes best illustrated by the small steps taken. Elizabeth, a mother of two high school boys, has recently completed college and reentered the workplace. When the children were younger she says she had been singularly devoted to their every need with few commitments outside of her family. As with many mid-life women in this study, she says that prior to returning to school she had never particularly cared for female companionship, and cared even less for her own "emotional side." She has always been extemely close to her sons and speaks of their and her husband's intellects with reverence. Now, however, her interests are expanding; she works in a human service agency with women she finds exciting and companionable. At times, as with many women who are in transition from full-time mother to full-time worker outside the home, she is forced to confront her own conflicting values about gender and power within her family.

The story she shares centers on the purchasing of her own television set. The old family set had broken the previous year and she, being "a very visual person who adores the movies more than anyone else in the family," had wanted to replace it at once. Her sons and her husband decided they did not want to replace the old one. They called for a family vote and Elizabeth was overruled. Even though she had voted against the decision she admits that she with her husband and sons began to feel quite virtuous and superior when she thought about all the time they had for other things, compared with their neighbors. Also she realized there was no longer the pull between television and homework for the boys.

After a year, however, she longed for the relaxation the television provided her after a tiring day at work. She also began to feel that she needed it *for* her work.

"At work I would hear about a lot of interesting and worthwhile sociological documentaries I really felt I ought to see. Also I was dealing with a public who watched all the time and there is a tremendous rapport to know what the latest soap opera is, even if I normally wouldn't watch it. It puts me on a level with them instead of up here."

Most influential were the comments of her new female friends concerning the power dynamics at work in her family:

"They were saying 'My God! You let that family of yours. . . . '

"I thought to myself — the hell with this — and I told the guys I wanted another vote. I lost again so I grumblingly acquiesced to this and told my friends, with what I again must confess was a kind of lurking pride in myself and my family for our democratic way of doing things, that that was that. But my friends were not impressed. They said: 'It isn't democratic at all. They are imposing their life-style on you. They don't have to watch it.' This, in fact, had been one of my sons' and husband's major reasons for not wanting it — if they were in the house they would be unable to resist watching it."

So, fortified once again by the advice of her new friends she went back home and said to her sons and husband:

"This isn't democracy. This is total dictatorship by you on me. I will lock the television up in my bedroom. I will watch it under the bedclothes. I won't allow anybody to see it. I'll do anything I can to help you not to watch it, but you should be able to exercise self-control and will power. In fact, I will be helping you to do so."

At this point, Elizabeth recalls, the family resisted more firmly than ever. "'Rubbish,' they responded. 'You're not having it.' I appealed to my husband and he refused to enter into it except to say 'of course, we are better off without it. Of course.'"

She then went back to her friends at work, and so it went like a seesaw for several more weeks. Finally she went to her husband and announced: "I am going to have one. I am going to go out and buy one."

"'Against the whole family's wishes! You will never get my approval,' he responded. 'All right, I will buy it without your approval,' I said. 'You do realize, Mom, that you will be ruining our chances to do well on our exams,' said my sons."

Elizabeth concluded that this was "the most naked emotional blackmail" she had ever encountered. She decided nothing would stop her now.

"I said 'Rubbish! Balls! I'm going to have it!' I decided to go the whole way and ordered the very best discount buy I could find — with color and everything. I phoned up the store from work to tell them I'd pick it up that evening. I set off in my car after work. But I could not drive to the store. I stopped the car by the side of the road three times. I was in an agony of torment. I was simply unable to go and buy it. I couldn't go against their will. I came home and I told them and they all laughed like crazy. They didn't feel any compassion for me at all. I thought and thought about it. I had another couple of talks, another set of injections from my friends, and three days later I went off and I got it."

Humorous or trivial as the story may strike us it symbolizes a new and vital direction for Elizabeth as she herself recognizes.

"It seems so minor now but it was a tremendously valuable decision for me I think. I took a resolve that I would deal with my own problems with the boys where we disagreed. I was prepared to take the responsibility for the decision and think as honestly as I could, Yes, this television is just for me. I don't find this easy. I've been so schooled to think that it's wrong to do something that is just for me. But it's coming."

MOTHERS AND SONS UNBOUNDING TOGETHER

Although the explicit focus of this study is on mothers, not sons, a cursory knowledge of contemporary male perspectives convinces us that most men still believe in and pursue the myth of the perfect mother whose life revolves around her son. This belief is said to be the prototype for all male dealings with women. John Updike reminds us that the entire topic of motherhood for men is

> intimidatingly large, and deep, and much mulled, especially in this post-Freudian century, when all blame and praise are assigned to the psychological matrix, the *alma* or *saeva mater* as the case may be, the dawning psyche's first and everlastingly internalized encounter, The Most Unforgettable — to quote Alexander Portnoy's autobiography — Character I've Met. (7)

Understandably the unbounding of mothers described above is frightening to many sons. But it need not be. Although from men's perspectives, "few things are harder, in this era so preoccupied with the monitoring of human relations, than to get to know one's mother as a person — to forgive her, in effect, for being one's mother," it is possible. Updike himself seems to be heading toward a new path. He describes how when he and his mother (he now in his early fifties and she approaching 80) talk on the telephone, he hears "how festive and limpid her wit is, and with what graceful, modest irony she illuminates every corner of her brave life." He laments that "all this for decades was muffled . . . behind the giant mask of motherhood." Finally now as they walk through the woods together he becomes aware that "the biological event that linked our two bodies seems further and further away, the mere beginning of a friendship." (8)

Friendships among mothers and sons are the capstones of mothers' struggles for balance in their lives. When mothers and sons can truly be friends we shall have come a long way toward a resolution of the gender question itself. As many of these stories have shown the script for mothers of sons as presently understood by both women and men almost precludes such affinity. Friendship must be "an extension of the self rather than a sacrifice of the self." (9) Its prerequisites include the ability to appreciate the integrity and identity of the other (including one's mother); an understanding of the complexity of assessing the needs of the other (including one's child); the knowledge that some pain and suffering is unavoidable; and the willingness to share or communicate openly. For the most part these prerequisites have not been a part of the rules of the game between mothers and sons.

Yet they have not been entirely absent either. In oral histories as in diaries and newspaper articles our discontents rather than our satisfactions unfortunately are most likely to be recorded. The complaints of mothers of sons predominate here. Bursting through the maze of ambivalent expressions of relating to sons as perceived by mothers, however, are also the buds of true friendships. To fail to acknowledge them would not only be an injustice to the mothers — it would also be missing the essential promise of the unbounding process itself.

Interspersed throughout the interviews are scenes of joyous celebrations, of warmly humorous anecdotes of daily living with sons, and of proud moments shared between people who deeply care for each other. For example, Serena captures the essence of true friendship as she talks about a special day she spent with her 22-year-old son Lauren in the high school in an underprivileged section of Chicago where he teaches math.

"This day was the high point of my motherhood. There was an atmosphere in the [class] room Lauren had created because he just has this unobtrusive way of walking among them. He teaches from within the class. He doesn't teach up front. There were kids who would come in very expressionless and they just stood there with their hands clenched. There was nothing but their bodies there and that was it. And Lauren, never judgmental or confrontational, would just walk over and say 'Why don't you get your book out so you don't fall behind?' or, 'Why don't you take notes because this will be on the test?'

"I noticed one person who just sat there passively and Lauren quietly said something to him and then I began to see this melting down process on the young man's face and towards the end of the class I saw him take his notebook out and actually start to write.

"Day after day Lauren is always trying to think how he can relate math to their world. He told me when he first began teaching it was troublesome. There were three groups: those who wanted to learn; those in between; and those who were very troublesome. Other teachers were making their classes manageable because they simply got rid of the troublemakers. Lauren found himself in a moral dilemma because to get rid of them meant forcing them to drop out of school and go on the streets. What a waste of human potential, he thought. But by keeping them in class he was taking valuable attention away from those who could maybe make it out of their situation.

"The fact that he had been wrestling with this affected me deeply as his mother. The thrilling thing was that he was having some limited success in that some of the kids in the middle group were beginning to do better and some in the troublesome group were starting to pass. I felt the same joy my son did.

"I sat there learning so much from Lauren. The valuing of each human being. I thought to myself, What a gifted teacher. This is a privilege to be here. Afterwards I told him that."

Also interspersed throughout the interviews are poignant expressions of ways in which mothers of sons are learning to support and understand each other. A mother tells of the comfort and advice she receives from her college sons as she struggles with Chemistry 101. Two mothers describe the warmth and love they and their gay sons share now that they have learned to accept that which they cannot change. A mother with her teenage sons who has sought the help of Al-Anon (a program for the families of alcoholics) describes how she and her sons grow strong together as they seek recovery from the ravages of a family torn apart by the alcoholism of the husband.

Working for better relationships with sons, some mothers have had to make difficult decisions based on deeply introspective explorations. One mother of three grown sons who, as she says of herself, has always "lived for her men," found herself resentfully mothering her son's son and decided to do something about it.

"I made a major decision. I really took a stand. And for a change I don't feel guilty. I feel good. It was something that was driving me down. I was becoming so resentful. It was getting so I could barely stand the sight of my son.

"When Pete [her son] was in the army he was really into the pot scene and he married someone who also was and they had a baby. When the baby was born she packed her clothes and left. The baby was four months old. Pete brought him home and I took care of him for three years. My son was having a good time while I was totally tied down. I finally told him and his girlfriend they could have three months together and then they were to take the child. They took him and it's worked out. I figured, hell, I'd raised my family and now it was my time. For the first time in my life I dared to say there were things I wanted to do. I feel really good about that decision. Pete and I are now closer than ever before. We both respect ourselves and each other."

Julia, a divorced mother of four who is a journalist, describes how she came to conclude that it was in the best interests of all concerned that her youngest son Kim, 15 at the time, live with his father.

"It was so complex. There were a lot of things going on. First, it seemed to be very important to Kim that his father really wanted him. He had been twelve at the time of separation and somehow he didn't feel he counted as much as the others. So on one level I think he really wanted his father to want him. Also I was really very sick for that whole year. I really had a very hard time physically and mentally. But most importantly, I knew that our relationship was very good — solid enough so there was no sense that Kim would feel rejection or a distance at all. After much agonizing thought I simply said, 'Kim, you may live where you wish. Wherever you choose to live you will always have two homes.'

"Blake [her ex-husband] thinks I have no sense of discipline at all — which I don't have much of. He has a different sense of things and actually I have to say I think Kim more than the other children wants discipline. Although to be perfectly honest I hate to admit it, he has done splendidly with Blake. Blake just has more traditional kinds of expectations than I have — to do homework, get to school on time, take the garbage out. These are not the fundamental things I value. Much as I hate to admit it I do think Blake gives Kim a sense of stability and order he seems to need right now.

"It just seems to have worked out so completely ideally since Kim made the decision to live with his father and come here weekends. There is nothing compulsory about it. He comes when he comes. We just have this really neat relationship. He has the key to my apartment and it turns out he loves to stop by with his friends at his mother's apartment in town. I know there is a kind of special pride in that. He and I are closer than we've ever been."

Unfortunately there are also the rare times when the building of a relationship between mothers and sons is not possible in this world that is not always just. This appeared to be at least temporarily the case for several of the women interviewed. One mother suffers episodes of mental illness where she becomes incompetent to care for her ten-year-old son. Her mother moves into her home at these times. Another is an alcoholic and has reluctantly placed her two young sons in the care of a foster home. One mother is preparing for a court hearing where her 11-year-old son will probably be removed from her home and placed in a rehabilitation center. (She has a husband in prison, four other children, and few coping skills of her own. The boy refuses to attend school, is frequently arrested for panhandling and shoplifting, and exhibits uncontrollably angry behavior toward his younger brothers and sisters.)

These three mothers weep with agonizing guilt over what they perceive to be their failures but they are coming to know their limitations and so are their sons. The unbounding of both mothers and sons requires an honest appraisal of limitations as well as the strengths of us all. (10)

THE RESPONSIBILITY QUESTION

Only when we can put to rest the all powerful mother stereotype and begin to see them as people with their own uniqueness struggling with conflicting values at a particular historical moment can we begin to understand. It is hoped that a closer look at the process of unbounding for mothers will assuage the fears of sons, freeing them from the dependency of a phantom. It is hoped that it also will serve to introduce them to women they can better understand and respect, a feat long thought to be impossible because of the centuries' long separation of men's and women's lives.

It is hoped that a closer look at the unbounding process will assuage the fears of women too. One mother puts it this way:

"I think we mothers of sons often just fall into the social expectations of the relationship rather than letting our relationships be unique in what they are. As women we live out others expectations — what we should do, shouldn't do. That is all we seem to be able to act on. We simply have to speak out so that we can break through all of that. If we break through to what is really right or true or best for us then we can have this fundamental sense of being there for our sons and also being free. And our sons can have that same sense of being there for us and also being free."

Women's search for the balance between selfhood and caring is contributing to the transformation of Western culture and the shattering of the mother-son myth. Experts disagree about the social implications of the changing American family in this time of transition, but few will deny that the changing role of women lies at the very core of it. Eli Ginsberg, the Columbia University economist, describes what is happening as "a revolution in the roles of women that will have an even greater impact than the rise of Communism and the development of nuclear energy," with secondary and tertiary consequences that are really unchartable. (11)

The desire for increasingly greater parity with men is, and increasingly will be in the future, the impetus for women speaking out on the efficacy of their responsibility for the well-being of sons. But anything that is unchartable is frightening. The tension, fear, and uncertainty about the family for both women and men is in large measure a reflection of the concern over who is going to be responsible if not *the* mother. Who is going to provide that haven in a heartless world? Who is going to mother the men of tomorrow? The question inevitably haunts us as we reflect on the mother-son relationships of the mothers in this study.

To attempt to answer the question is nothing less than to take on the ageless challenge of how both women and men can lead fuller lives. Of course there are no easy answers, no wondrous blueprint. Women, men, sons, and daughters are and will always be searching for ways to balance the commitments of their daily lives. The modest objective of this study, given the egocentricity of most people's accounts of their experiences and the "pre-predictiveness" noted for oral history in the Introduction, has been to move the search forward by listening to mothers of sons speaking out so that we can begin to ask new questions, explore new processes.

Our conclusions based on these women's stories assuredly cast doubt on Freud's characterization that the mother-son relationship is one of "the purest examples of unchanging tenderness, undisturbed by egoistic consideration." Women are telling us they are often overwhelmed by the mothering responsibility itself; made to feel guilty about expectations they cannot possibly meet; and confused as to what constitutes "good" mothering, particularly when it comes to the raising of sons.

As Betty Friedan pointed out several decades ago, the social sciences, greatly influenced by Freud, have been part of the problem rather than the solution. "Instead of destroying the old prejudices that restricted women's lives social science in America merely gave them new authority. By a curious circular process, the insights of psychology and anthropology and sociology, which should have been powerful weapons to free women . . . canceled each other out, trapping women in dead center." (12) Too much responsibility has been placed on mothers, even after the children become adults. They have been treated, even by some feminist writers, as though they were an independent variable with Godlike powers.

Who, then, is going to mother the men of tomorrow? I believe the answer is very much in process. The responsibility of mothering must be shared so that both genders can have commitment to work, to citizenship, to social justice, to personal love, to family, and to household. This requires that we confront the inevitability of painful conflicts of daily living — the juggling of care for children, demands of career, in a nonsexist society. This requires that we continue to explore the ways in which children and adults of both sexes develop and change over their life span with respect to their uniqueness as well as their commonalities. (13) Most importantly, this requires that we confront the larger structural questions embedded in the history of a public policy that has institutionalized women's oppression.

Mothering must be shared. The mothering of sons must be the responsibility of mothers, fathers, sons themselves, siblings, aunts, uncles, grandparents, friends, and, most importantly, a more humane state. I am an optimist at heart. I firmly believe that when the sons of tomorrow are the responsibility of the many instead of the one they will grow freer, stronger, and more caring, and so will their mothers.

NOTES

1.   Michael Harrington, *Taking Sides: The Education of a Militant Mind* (New York: Holt, Rinehart & Winston, 1985), as quoted in the New York *Times Book Review,* Jan. 12, 1986, p. 19.

2.   William James, *The Varieties of Religious Experience* (New York: Penquin Books, 1982), p. 9.

3.   Feminist scholarship has been characterized by a wonderfully creative growth process that is especially sensitive to new tensions, a sensitivity that derives from its poignantly open analyses of the experiences of women, women of the past as well as the present. Theoretical shifts have been constant and quite natural to this open-minded, open-ended process. Feminist scholars, as all scholars ideally should, have dared to challenge even themselves. For the most part feminist scholarship in the 1960s and 1970s has emphasized the similarities of men and women and has fought against societal stereotyping of their differences. Its direction in the 1980s, as we have noted in the work of Carol Gilligan, has shifted, however. It is toward a belief, not unlike that of nineteenth-century feminists, that women because of their greater connectedness with others are more caring and in a sense morally superior to men.

4.   Ann Oakley, *Taking It Like a Woman* (London: Fontana Paperbacks, 1984), p. 123.

5.   Ibid., p. 197.

6.   Of the women interviewed 25 were employed part time, 49 full time, 5 retired, and 41 not employed at time of interview.

7.   John Updike, "The Most Unforgettable Character I've Ever Met," *Vogue* (November, 1984), p. 441.

8.   Ibid.

9.   M. Scott Peak, *The Road Less Traveled* (New York: Simon and Schuster, 1978), p. 116.

10.   Phyllis Chesler in *Mothers on Trial: The Battle for Children and Custody* (New York: McGraw-Hill, 1985), convincingly presents stories from some mothers who because of paternal custody challenges have been victims of gross abuses of

justice. She also convincingly argues that mothers as primary caretakers should generally be given preference. She, however, overstates her argument. Clearly it is not always in the interests of the child that the mother be granted custody.

11. New York *Times,* Nov. 29, 1977, p. 28.

12. Betty Friedan, *The Feminine Mystique* (New York: Dell, 1963), p. 117.

13. " . . . There are important growth changes across the life span from birth to death, many individuals retain a great capacity for change, and the consequences of the events of early childhood are continually transformed by later experiences, making the course of human development more open than many have believed," write Orville G. Brim, Jr., and Jerome Kagan, in "Constancy and Change: A View of the Issues," in *Constancy and Change in Human Development,* ed. Orville G. Brim, Jr., and Jerome Kagan (Cambridge, Mass.: Harvard University Press, 1980), pp. 1–25.

Bibliography

Allport, Gordon W., ed. and interpreter. *Letters from Jenny*. New York: Harcourt Brace Jovanovich, 1965.

Andry, R. "Paternal and Maternal Roles and Delinquency." *Deprivation of Maternal Care*. Geneva, WHO Public Health Papers, no. 14, 1962.

Arcana, Judith. *Every Mother's Son: The Role of Mothers in the Making of Men*. Garden City, N.Y.: Doubleday, 1983.

Aries, Philippes. *Centuries of Childhood*. New York: Knopf, 1963.

Armitage, Susan H. "The Next Step." *Frontiers* 7 (1983): 3–8.

Aronowitz, Stanley. *False Promises*. New York: McGraw-Hill, 1973.

Badinter, Elizabeth. *Mother Love*. New York: Macmillan, 1980.

Baker, Russell. *Growing Up*. New York: Congdon and Weed, 1982.

Banay, Ralph S. *Youth in Despair*. New York: Coward-McCann, 1948.

Bateson, G. *Steps to an Ecology of Mind*. New York: Ballantine, 1972.

Bateson, G., Don D. Jackson, Jay Haley, and John Weakland. "Toward a Theory of Schizophrenia." *Beyond the Double Bind*. Edited by Milton M. Berger. New York: Brunner/Mazel, 1978.

Bayley, Nancy, and E. S. Schaefer. "Relationships Between Socio-economic Variables and the Behavior of Mothers Toward Young Children." *Journal of Genetic Psychology* 96 (1960): 61–77.

Beauvoir, Simone de. *The Second Sex*. New York: Random House, 1974.

Bell, Alan P., Martin S. Weinberg, and Sue Kiefer Hammersmith. *Sexual Preference: Its Development in Men and Women*. Bloomington: Indiana University Press, 1981.

Bennett, James. *Oral History and Delinquency: The Rhetoric of Criminology*. Chicago: University of Chicago Press, 1981.

Benston, Margaret. "The Political Economy of Women's Liberation." *Monthly Review* 21 (September 1969).

Berkner, Lutz K. "Recent Research on the History of the Family in Western Europe." *Journal of Marriage and the Family* 35 (August 1973).

Bernard, Jesse. *The Future of Marriage.* New York: Penquin Books, 1973.

_____. *The Future of Motherhood.* New York: Penquin Books, 1975.

Bernheim, Kayla F., and Richard R. J. Lewine. *Schizophrenia: Symptoms, Causes, Treatments.* New York: W. W. Norton, 1979.

Bibring, Grete. "On the 'Passing of the Oedipus Complex' in a Matriarchal Family Setting." *Drives, Affects, and Behavior: Essays in Honor of Marie Bonaparte.* Edited by R. M. Lowenstein. New York: International Universities Press, 1953.

Bieber, Irwing, et al. *Homosexuality, A Psychoanalytical Study.* New York: Basic Books, 1962.

Boudreau, Frances A., Roger S. Sennott, and Michele Wilson, *Sex Roles and Social Patterns.* New York: Praeger, 1986.

Braverman, Harry. *Labor and Monopoly Capitalism: The Degradation of Work in the Twentieth Century.* New York: Monthly Review Press, 1974.

Brim, Orville, Jr., and Jerome Kagan, eds. *Constancy and Change in Human Development.* Cambridge, Mass.: Harvard University Press, 1980.

Brock-Utne, Birgit. *Educating for Peace: A Feminist Perspective.* New York: Pergamon Press, 1985.

Brown, Norman O. *Love's Body.* New York: Vintage Books, 1968.

Brownmiller, Susan. *Against Our Will: Men, Women and Rape.* New York: Simon and Schuster, 1975.

Carter, Elizabeth, and Monica McGoldrick. *The Family Life Cycle.* New York: Gardner, 1980.

Cherry, Laurence, and Rona Cherry. "Another Way of Looking at the Brain." New York *Times Magazine,* June 9, 1985, p. 56.

Chesler, Phyllis. *Mothers on Trial: The Battle for Children and Custody.* New York: McGraw-Hill, 1985.

Chodorow, Nancy. *The Reproduction of Mothering: Psychoanalysis and the Sociology of Gender.* Berkeley: University of California Press, 1978.

Chodorow, Nancy, and Susan Contratto. "The Fantasy of the Perfect Mother." *Rethinking the Family.* Edited by Barrie Throne and Marilyn Yalom. New York: Longman, 1982.

Coles, Robert. *Irony in the Mind's Life: Essay on Novels by James Agee, Elizabeth Bowen, and George Elliot.* New York: New Directions, 1974.

Dalla Costa, Mariarosa, and Selma James. *The Power of Women and the Subversion of the Community.* Bristol, Eng.: Falling Wall Press, 1972.

Dally, Ann. *Inventing Motherhood.* London: Burnett, 1982.

Deleuze, Gilles, and Felix Guattari. *Anti-Oedipus: Capitalism and Schizophrenia.* New York: Viking Press, 1977.

Devereux, G. "Why Oedipus Killed Laius." *International Journal of Psycho-Analysis* 34 (1953).

Dinnerstein, Dorothy. *The Mermaid and the Minotaur.* New York: Harper & Row, 1976.

Ehrenreich, Barbara. "A Feminist's View of the New Man." New York *Times Magazine,* May 20, 1984.

____. *The Hearts of Men.* Garden City: Anchor Press/Doubleday, 1983.

Eisenhower, Dwight D. "This Country Needs Universal Military Training." *Readers Digest,* vol. 89 (September 1966).

Erikson, Erik. "The First Psychoanalyst." *Yale Review,* Autumn, 1965.

Fenichel, O. *The Psychoanalytic Theory of Neurosis.* London: Kegan Paul, 1945.

Forcey, Linda Rennie. "Making of Men in the Military: Perspectives from Mothers." *Women's Studies International Forum* 7 (1984): 477–86.

____. "Personality in Politics: The Commitment of a Suicide." Ph.D. diss. State University of New York at Binghamton, 1978.

Freud, Sigmund. *A General Introduction to Psychoanalysis.* New York: Garden City Books, 1943.

____. *New Introductory Lectures on Psychoanalysis.* vol. 22, *Standard Edition of the Complete Psychological Works.* London: Hogarth Press, 1933.

____. *New Introductory Lectures on Psychoanalysis.* Edited by James Strachey. New York: Norton, 1961.

____. "The Interpretation of Dreams." *The Basic Writings of Sigmund Freud.* Edited by A. A. Brill. New York: Random House, 1938.

Friedan, Betty. *The Feminine Mystique.* New York: Dell, 1963.

Friedman, Bruce Jay. *A Mother's Kisses.* New York: Simon and Schuster, 1964.

Fromm, Erich. *The Art of Loving.* New York: Perennial, 1974.

Galenson, Eleanor. "Scientific Proceedings — Panel Reports." Panels on the Psychology of Women, Annual Meeting of the American Psychoanalytic Association, 1974. *Journal of the American Psychoanalytic Association* 24: 141–60.

Gelles, R. J. *The Violent Home.* Beverly Hills: Sage, 1972.

Gilligan, Carol. *In A Different Voice.* Cambridge, Mass.: Harvard University Press, 1982.

Gimenez, Martha E. "Structuralist Marxism on 'The Woman Question.'" *Science and Society* 42, no. 3 (Fall 1978).

Gluck, Sherna. "What's So Special About Women? Women's Oral History." *Frontiers* 2 (1977): 1–17.

Glueck, S., and E. Glueck. *Unraveling Juvenile Delinquency.* New York: Commonwealth, 1950.

Glueck, Sheldon and Eleanor. *Family Environment and Delinquency.* London: Routledge & Kegan Paul, 1962.

Gordon, Michael, ed. *The American Family in Social-Historical Perspective.* 2d. ed. New York: St. Martin's Press, 1978.

Greenburg, Dan. *How to Be a Jewish Mother.* Los Angeles: Price, Stern, Sloan, 1964.

Greer, Germaine. *Sex and Destiny: The Politics of Human Fertility.* New York: Harper & Row, 1984.

Hall, G. Stanley. *Adolescence: Its Psychology and Its Relations to Physiology, Anthropology, Sociology, Sex, Crime, Religion and Education.* New York: Appleton, 1904.

Harrington, Michael. *Taking Sides: The Education of a Militant Mind.* New York: Holt, Rinehart & Winston, 1985.

Hart, John, and Diane Richardson. *The Theory and Practice of Homosexuality.* London: Routledge and Kegan Paul, 1981.

Heilbrun, Carolyn. "Hers." New York *Times,* Feb. 5, 1981, p. C2.

Hirsch, Steven R., and Julian P. Leff. *Abnormalities in Parents of Schizophrenics.* London: Oxford University Press, 1975.

James, William. *The Varieties of Religious Experience.* New York: Penquin Books, 1982.

Jones, Ernest. *Hamlet and Oedipus.* New York: Doubleday, 1954.

Kasanin, J., E. Knight, and P. Sage. "The Parent-Child Relationship in Schizophrenia." *Journal of Mental Disease* 79 (1934): 249–63.

Kazin, Alfred. *A Walker in the City.* New York: Harcourt and Brace, 1951.

Keniston, Kenneth. *The Uncommitted: Alienated Youth in American Society.* New York: Dell, 1960.

Klein, Carole. *Mothers and Sons.* Boston: Houghton Mifflin, 1984.

Komarovsky, Mirra. *Blue-Collar Marriage.* New York: Random House, 1962.

Landis, Judson T., and Mary G. Landis. *Building a Successful Marriage.* New York: Prentice-Hall, 1953.

Lasch, Christopher. *The Culture of Narcissism.* New York: Warner Books, 1979.

____. *Haven in a Heartless World.* New York: Basic Books, 1977.

Lawrence, D. H. *Sons and Lovers.* London: Duckworth, 1913.

Lazarre, Jane. *The Mother Knot.* New York: Dell, 1976.

Leslie, Gerald R. *The Family in Social Context.* New York: Oxford University Press, 1973.

Levy, David M. "Maternal Overprotection." *Psychiatry* 1 (1938): 561–91; 2 (1939): 99–128.

____. "Maternal Overprotection and Rejection." *Arch. Neurol. Psychiat.* 25 (1931).

Lidz, T., S. Fleck, and A. Cornelison, "The Mothers of Schizophrenic Patients." In *Schizophrenia and the Family.* New York: International Universities Press, 1965.

Macoby, Eleanor, and Carol Jacklin. *The Psychology of Sex Differences*. Stanford: Stanford University Press, 1974.

Manchester, William. *American Caesar: Douglas MacArthur, 1880–1964*. New York: Dell, 1978.

McCord, J., W. McCord, and E. Thurber. "Some Effects of Paternal Absence on Male Children." *Journal of Abnormal and Social Psychology* 64 (1962): 361–69.

McCord, J., and W. McCord with I. Zola. *Origins of Crime*. New York: Columbia University Press, 1969.

Miller, Jean Baker. *Toward a New Psychology of Women*. Boston: Beacon Press, 1976.

Mills, C. Wright. *White Collar*. New York: Oxford University Press, 1951.

Mitchell, Juliet. *Psychoanalysis and Feminism: Freud, Reich, Laing and Women*. New York: Random House, 1974.

Molyneux, Maxine, "Beyond the Housework Debate." *New Left Review* 116 (July-August 1979).

Nisbet, Robert. *Prejudices: A Philosophical Dictionary*. Cambridge, Mass.: Harvard University Press, 1982.

Oakley, Ann. "Interviewing Women: A Contradiction in Terms." In *Doing Feminist Research*, edited by Helen Roberts. London: Routledge & Kegan Paul, 1981.

____. *Subject Women*. New York: Pantheon, 1981.

____. *Taking It Like a Woman*. London: Fontana Paperbacks, 1984.

Oates, Joyce Carol. *Expensive People*. New York: Vanguard, 1968.

Odets, Clifford. "Awake and Sing!" In *Masters of Modern Drama*, edited by Haskell M. Block and Robert G. Shedd. New York: Random House, 1962.

Olivier, Christiane. *Les Enfants de Jocaste*. Paris: Editions Deroel/Gonthier, 1980.

Olsen, Paul. *Sons and Mothers*. New York: Fawcett Crest, 1981.

Olsen, Tillie. *Silences*. New York: Dell, 1978.

Peck, M. Scott. *The Road Less Traveled*. New York: Simon and Schuster, 1978.

Pleck, Joseph H. *The Myth of Masculinity.* Cambridge Mass.: MIT Press, 1981.

Rapp, Rayna, Ellen Ross, and Renate Bridenthal. "Examining Family History," *Feminist Studies* 5, no. 1 (Spring 1979).

Rich, Adrienne. *Of Woman Born.* New York: W. W. Norton, 1976.

____. *On Lies, Secrets and Silence.* New York: W. W. Norton, 1979.

Roth, Philip. *Portnoy's Complaint.* New York: Bantam Books, 1970.

Rubenfeld, Seymour. *Family of Outcasts: A New Theory of Delinquency.* New York: The Free Press, 1965.

Rubin, Josephine. "Women and Peace." *Whole Earth Papers,* vol. 1, no. 6 (Spring 1978).

Rubin, Lillian Breslow. *Intimate Strangers.* New York: Harper and Row, 1983.

____. *Worlds of Pain: Life in the Working Class Family.* New York: Basic Books, 1976.

Sanua, Victor D. "Sociological Factors in Families of Schizophrenics: A Review of the Literature." *Psychiatry* 24 (1961): 247.

Sapiro, Virginia. *Women in American Society.* Palo Alto, Ca.: Mayfield, 1986.

Sartre, Jean-Paul. *Existential Psychoanalysis.* Chicago: Henry Regnery, 1962.

Secombe, Wally. "Housework under Capitalism." *New Left Review,* no. 83 (January-February 1975).

Seifer, Nancy. *Nobody Speaks for Me: Self-Portraits of American Working Class Women.* New York: Simon and Schuster, 1976.

Silvermann, I. J., and S. Dinitz. "Compulsive Masculinity and Delinquency." *Criminology* 11 (1974): 499–515.

Slater, Philip E. *The Glory of Hera: Greek Mythology and the Greek Family.* Boston: Beacon Press, 1968.

____. *The Pursuit of Loneliness: American Culture at the Breaking Point.* Boston: Beacon Press, 1972.

Smith-Rosenberg, Carroll. "The Female World of Love and Ritual: Relations Between Women in Nineteenth-Century America." *Signs* 1 (1975): 1–29.

Sophocles. "Oedipus Tyrannus." *The Complete Tragedies*. Translated by David Grene. Chicago: University of Chicago Press, 1959.

Stewart, Harold. "Jocasta's Crimes." *International Journal of Psychoanalysis* 42 (1961): 424–30.

Stonequist, Everett. V. *Marginal Man*. New York: Charles Scribner's Sons, 1937.

Swerdlow, Amy, Renate Bridenthal, Joan Kelly, and Phyllis Vine. *Household and Kin: Families in Flux*. New York: Feminist Press and McGraw-Hill, 1980.

Thompson, N. L., et al. "Parent-Child Relationships and Sexual Identity in Male and Female Homosexuals and Heterosexuals." *Journal of Abnormal Psychology* 73 (1973): 201–6.

Thorne, Barrie, and Marilyn Yalom, eds. *Rethinking the Family*. New York: Longman, 1982.

Trebilcot, Joyce, ed. *Mothering: Essays in Feminist Theory*. Totowa, N. J.: Rowman & Allanheld, 1983.

Updike, John. "The Most Unforgettable Character I've Ever Met." *Vogue* (November 1984).

Van Der Sterran, H. A. "The 'King Oedipus' of Sophocles." *International Journal of Psycho-Analysis* 33 (1952).

Vellikovsky, Immanuel. *Oedipus and Akhnaton: Myth and History*. New York: Garden City Books, 1952.

Vogel, Lise. "The Earthly Family." *Radical America 7*, nos. 4 and 5 (July-October 1973).

Wandor, M., ed. *The Body Politic: Writings from the Women's Liberation Movement in Britain 1969–72*. London: Stage I, 1973.

West, D. J. *Homosexuality Re-examined*. Minneapolis: University of Minnesota Press, 1977.

Whiting, John W. M. "Sorcery, Sin, and the Superego: A Cross-Cultural Study of Some Mechanisms of Social Control." *Cross-Cultural Approaches: Readings in Comparative Research*. Edited by Clellan S. Ford. New Haven: Human Relations Area Files, 1959.

Wilensky, Harold L. "Mass Society and Mass Culture: Interdependence or Independence." *American Sociological Review* 29 (1964): 173–97.

Wilson, E. O. *On Human Nature.* Cambridge, Mass.: Harvard University Press, 1978.

____. *Sociobiology: The New Synthesis.* Cambridge, Mass.: Harvard University Press, 1975.

Winnicott, D. W. *The Child, The Family, and the Outside World.* Middlesex, Eng.: Harmondsworth, 1961.

Witmer, H. "The Childhood Personality and Parent-Child Relationships of Dementia Praecox and Manic Depressive Patients." *Smith College Studies on Social Work* 4, pp. 290–377.

Wylie, Philip. *Generation of Vipers.* New York: Farrar & Rhinehart, 1942.

Index

adolescence, 6, 44, 49–50, 85, 104
age: of mothers, 10, 13, 74, 75, 104, 108, 125–26; of sons, 10, 13, 19, 22 (*see also* adolescence; childhood; mothers, middle years)
alcohol (*see* drug and alcohol abuse)
Allport, Gordon W., 6
ambivalence, 22, 30, 32, 60, 86, 87, 92–93, 108, 138
American Psychological Association, 22
anger, 6, 14, 53, 60, 86, 91, 113, 128, 141
Arcana, Judith, 28, 110
Aries, Philippe, 44
army, 117–20, 122–23 (*see also* military)

Baker, Russell, 65
Beauvoir, Simone de, 29–30, 32, 48, 59, 63, 71, 117–18, 119, 137, 138 (*see also* daughters, happiness)
Bennett, James, 7
Bernard, Jesse, 31–32, 44–45
biology, 4–5, 25
black women, 47, 66, 72, 137, 140–41
black men, 132
Boston Strangler, 23
Brock-Utne, Birgit, 117
Brown, Norman O., 21

capitalism, 28, 43
child support, 98, 103
childhood: of sons, 18, 32, 44–45, 63, 104; of mothers, 120, 121, 128 (*see also* Aries, Philippe; Oedipus)
Churchill, Winston, 77
Chodorow, Nancy, 33–34, 35–36, 46, 81, 138
class, 4, 10–11, 27, 28, 49, 67–68, 75, 108, 114, 119, 130, 137, 138 (*see also* middle class, upper class, working class)
Colette, 29

commitment, 104, 105, 110–12, 139
communication, 81–82, 83–85, 95, 100, 121, 126–27 (*see also* daughters; Gilligan, Carol; peacemakers)
confrontations, 14, 89–95 (*see also* drug and alcohol abuse)

daughters, 2, 3, 4, 29, 45, 108; communication with, 74–75, 82, 96, 97, 138, 140 (*see also* illness); connectedness with, 30, 31, 32, 33–34, 35–36, 46, 73 (*see also* Beauvoir, Simone de; Chodorow, Nancy; Friedan, Betty; Gilligan, Carol; Rich, Adrienne); expectations of fathers, 148; expectations of mothers, 74, 75–77, 138; preference for, 52, 74
daughters-in-law, 102, 108, 113–15, 138
death, 1, 49, 97, 118, 131; of husband, 69; of son, 5–6, 68–69 (*see also* suicide)
Dinnerstein, Dorothy, 32–33, 42
divorce, 63, 71; of mothers, 55–56, 89, 96, 98–100, 104, 147; of sons, 53, 113, 147
double bind theory, 24–25
drug and alcohol abuse: of daughter-in-law, 113–14; of husbands, 121, 141–42, 147; of mothers, 69–70, 92–93, 148; of sons, 67, 68–71, 83, 91–94, 106–7, 120, 121, 126, 127

education: of mothers, 9, 10, 11, 140–41; of sons, 67, 107, 119–20, 121, 123, 126, 132, 133, 134 (*see also* school, military)
Ehrenreich, Barbara, 110
Eisenhower, Dwight D., 131
employment (*see* work)
Erikson, Erik, 6, 35
Every Mother's Son (*see* Arcana, Judith)

163

Manchester, William)
MacArthur, Pinky (*see* Manchester, William)
marines, 130, 133–34
marriage: mother/son, 20–21; of mothers, 55, 56, 59, 68, 110, 121, 125, 128, 140; of sons, 53, 57, 108, 110, 114, 123; sexual problems, 98
masculinity, 23, 24, 27, 33, 43, 46–47, 110, 138
mental illness: mothers, 148; sons, 24–25, 50, 122 (*see also* schizophrenia)
middle class, 11, 22, 23, 48, 49, 53, 66, 67–68, 70, 74
military: attitudes of mothers, 13, 117–34; recruitment literature, 132–34
motherhood (institution of), 2, 23, 28, 29, 31–32, 34, 46, 59
mothers: controlling, 54, 56, 57, 78–79; definition of, 4; "good" mothers, 35, 43, 45, 46, 65, 137, 138, 150; middle years, 10, 13, 59, 75, 104, 125–26, 142; powerful, 27, 28, 36, 43, 46, 47, 54, 149; schizo-phrenogenic, 24 (*see also* age, black, class, drug and alcohol abuse, education, Hispanic, Jewish, illness, lesbian, myths about mothers, peacemakers, school, single mothers, work, welfare)
Mothers and Sons (*see* Klein, Carole)
mothers-in-law, 102, 113
myths about mothers, 15, 17–21, 22, 29, 36, 43, 65, 66, 71, 117–18, 119, 139, 145

navy, 126, 127–28, 131–32
narcissism, 1, 22–23
Nobody Speaks for Me (*see* Seifer, Nancy)

Oakley, Ann, 1, 8, 139
Oates, Joyce Carol, 58
Odets, Clifford, 103

Oedipus, 18–21, 66
Oedipus complex, 19–20, 34, 45
Oedipus myth, 17–21, 103 (*see also* myths about mothers)
Of Woman Born (*see* Rich, Adrienne)
Officer and a Gentleman, 130
Olsen, Paul, 43, 63, 118–19
Olsen, Tillie, 17
oral history, 3, 8, 12, 13, 74, 145–46, 150

patriarchy, 23, 28, 46, 82
peacemakers, 85–89, 91–94, 137
Peck, M. Scott, 95
perception (definition), 4
phenomenology, 6, 7, 8
Portnoy's Complaint (*see* Roth, Philip)
poverty, 66, 70, 120, 121, 128
pregnancy, 57, 74
psychoanalysis, 17, 18, 20, 24, 32, 33, 34, 66
psychology, 22, 24, 26, 32–37, 58, 59, 126, 139, 150

racism, 67
Reagan administration, 85
reality problems, 66–67, 68, 119
reification, 2, 36–37
relationship (definition of), 4
religion, 69, 138
Reproduction of Mothering (*see* Chodorow, Nancy)
responsibility: definition, 4; of mothers, 1, 2, 3–4, 7, 13, 14, 15, 23, 27, 28, 29–33, 36, 42–60, 65, 82, 85, 89, 94, 99–100, 107, 137, 138, 140, 144, 149–51
Rich, Adrienne, 28–29, 37, 46, 81, 82–83, 119
Rockefeller, Happy, 97
Roth, Philip, 14, 63–64, 67, 68
Rowbotham, Sheila, 36
Ruben, Lillian Breslow, 3, 115

Sartre, Jean-Paul, 29
schizophrenia, 22, 24–25

About the Author

Linda Rennie Forcey is Associate Professor at the State University of New York at Binghamton. She received her BS and MA in History from Columbia University and (while raising, with the help of her husband, three sons and three daughters) her Ph.D. in Political Science from the State University of New York at Binghamton. She teaches in the Career and Interdisciplinary Studies Division of the School of General Studies and Professional Education where she also coordinates a Masters in Social Sciences Program and a Peace Studies Education Center. She is currently engaged in research on interdisciplinary approaches to the study of peace.